John Heydon

## The Wise-Mans Crown

The glory of the rosie-cross - shewing the wonderful power of nature, with the full

discovery of the true coelum terrae, or first matter of metals, and their

preparations into incredible medicines or elixirs

John Heydon

**The Wise-Mans Crown**
*The glory of the rosie-cross - shewing the wonderful power of nature, with the full discovery of the true coelum terrae, or first matter of metals, and their preparations into incredible medicines or elixirs*

ISBN/EAN: 9783337255756

Printed in Europe, USA, Canada, Australia, Japan

Cover: Foto ©Andreas Hilbeck / pixelio.de

More available books at **www.hansebooks.com**

# The Wise—Mans Crown :

## OR, THE

# GLORY

## Of the

# Rosie-Cross.

### SHEWING

## The Wonderful Power of Nature,

with the full discovery of the true *Cælum Terræ*, or first Matter of Metals, and their Preparations into incredible Medicines or Elixirs that cure all Diseases in Young or Old: With the *Regio Lucis*, and holy Houshold of *Rosie Crucian* Philosophers.

---

### Communicated to the World

## By JOHN HEYDON, Gent.

### A Servant of GOD, and Secretary to Nature.

---

Ἐις ἱμέ τις ὁρέων ἰνσιδης ἔσω. (i. e.)

*He that looketh upon my Books, let him learn to be religious.*

---

### LONDON:

Printed for the Author; and are to be sold by *Samuel Speed* at the Rainbow in Fleetstreet. 1 6 6 4.

To the Moft Excellently Accomplished the truly honourable
learned wife vertuous &c.

# Bevis Lloyd Efq.

Eternal
Health be wifhed.

Would have you know, that I
love and honor you beyond ex-
preffion and fhall ferve you in
Art and Nature to my power, I
have prefumed to make you one
in the number of my Noble Patrons, becaufe I
hear the wickednefs of fome Pulpit Polititi-
ans inceffantly rageing againft my perfon
which they never faw, nor perhaps will fee,
thefe fophiftical Sicophants contend againft
me continually with bitter hatred, envy and
Malice, without any provocation on my part

B                                              one

one very proudly with a full mouth and loud
voice aſperſed me with Atheiſme in St. Pauls
Church in his morning Sermon the eight of
May, before the Lord Mayor and others, A-
mongſt a promiſcuous people, Railing againſt
the Roſie Crucians, who Art and Nature united, Others in Coffee diſcourſe and ſtinking
ſmoak of Tobacco did fill the ears of the Ignorant with my infamy others in publique
and private aſſemblies, I bear do inſtigate
the Dukes Princes and Peers of England &c
againſt me, But my Religion being publiſhed.
I would have you know my Philoſoply is to
know God himſelf, the worker of all things, &
to paſs into him by a whole Image of likeneſs
(as by an Eſſential Contract and bond) where
by we may be transformed and made as God
As the Lord ſpake concerning Moſes, ſaying
I have made thee the God of Pharoah, this i
the true Roſie Crucian Philoſophy of wonder
ful works, that they underſtand not, the Ke
thereof is the intellect: for by how much high
er things we underſtand with ſo much th
ſublimer vertues are we endowed, and ſ
much greater things do work, and that mor
eaſily and efficatiouſly But our intellect bein
included in the Corruptible fleſh, unleſs it ſha
exceed the way of the fleſh and obtain a pre

P

per Nature, cannot be united to these vertues
(for like to like) And is in searching into
the Rosie Crucian secrets of God and Nature
altogether in efficatious; for it is no easie
thing for us to ascend to the Heavens, for how
shall he that hath lost himself in Morral Dust
and ashes, find God. How shall he apprehend
spiritual things that is swallowed up in flesh
and bloud, can man see God and live, what
fruit shall a grain of Corn bear if it be
not first dead, for we must dye, I say dye to the
world, and to the flesh, and all sences and to
the whole man Animal, who would enter into
these closets of secrets, Not because the body
is seperated from the soul, but because the soul
leaves the body, of which death S. Paul wrot
to the Collossians : ye are dead and your life
is hid with Christ : And elsewhere he speaks
more clearly of himself, I know a Man, whether in the body or out of the body I cannot tel,
God knows, caught up unto the third heaven
&c. I say by this death pretious in the sight of
God we must dye which happens to few : and
not always, for very few whom God loves, and
are vertuous are made so happy. And first
those that are born, not of flesh and blood,
but of God? secondly those that are dignified
by the blessed assistance of Angels and Genii

B 2

the

the Power of Nature Influence of Planets, and the Heavens and vertues of the figures and Ideas at their birth, now this I humbly intreat you, that you be not mistaken concerning me as if I at any time having received such divine things should boast of them to you, or should arrogate any such thing to my self, or could hope to have them granted to me, Although I have hitherto kept my self unmarryed and free from the company of a woman, yet I have been a souldier following the Armies of the King, and in other Countries consecrated with mans bloud, and exposed to all the blasts of inconstant fortune, & being crossed in my flesh in the world and worldly afairs and therefore could not obtain the sublime Gifts of the Immortal God. But I would be accounted a director, who always waiting at the dores shews to others which way they must go, And here I present my self your most humble servant and honourer

May the 9th
1664 D 5 bo
A. M.

*John Heydon.*

# An Apologue for an Epilogue

ABout the year 1648 we Studied
Aftronancy and Geomancy, and writ
the *Harmony of the World* in two Books,
the firft Printed for *Mr. Brome* with the
*Temple* of *Wifdome* at his houfe in *Ivy-Lane*,
The *Holy Guide, Elhavareuna*, being an
Introduction to the *Rofie Crucian* philofophy, and diverfly Compiled in thefe
Books, in fhort words, yet fufficient for
thofe who are wife; fome of thefe things
are written Methodically, fome without
order pur pofely fome things are delivered
by fragments, fome things are even hid
and left for the fearch of the wife, who
more acutely contemplating thefe things
which are written, and diligently fearching
(the *Harmony* of the *World*, the *Temple* of
*Wifdome*, and the *Holy Guide*) may obtain
the Compleat rudiments of the *Rofie
Crucian* Philofophy and alfo infallible
experiments: and if you defire to ftudy
thefe Books, keep filence and Conftantly
conceal within the fecret clofet of your
Religous breaft, fo holy a determination;

B                                    for

for ( as Taphthartharath faith ) to publish to the knowledge of many an Art wholly filled with fo great Majefty of the Deity, is a fign of an Irreligious fpirit; and Divine *Plato* Commanded that holy and fecret mifteries fhould not be made publique to the people, *Pythagoras* and *Prophiry* confecrated their followers to a religious Silence, The *Rofie Crucians* with a certain terible authority of religion, do exact an oath of filence from thofe they initiate to the Arts of Aftromancy Geomancy & Telefmaticall Images, becaufe by them the dead are raifed to life, by them they alter change and amend bodies, cure the defeafed prolong Life, preferve Health, renew youth in old folke, make dwarfs grow great men, make fools and Madmen wife and vertuous, deftroy the power of writchs, by thefe Arts they make men fortunate in play, law fuits love, victory over enimies, in Horfe Races in Gameing, in *Merchandize* and at fea, filencing the violent waves, by thefe Arts they know all things and refolve all manner of queftions prefent or to come, as faith *Beata*.

YOu that admirers are of vertue, stay
Consider well what I to you shall say,
But you, that sacred laws contemn, prophane
Away from hence, return no more again,
But thou O my Engenius whose mind is high
Observe my words & read them with thine eye,
And them within thy sacred breast repone
And in thy journy thinke of God alone,
The Author of all things that cannot die.
Of whom we now shall Treat ———
And Engenius The odidactus Proclaims
Beata Pulchra *comes, hence, hence, all ye*
(*prophane*
*Theodidatus cryes, & from her grove refrain.*

Now in celebrating the holy misteries
of *Hester Heaton,* and *Beata Pulchra* they
only were admitted to be initiated, *Eugenius*
*Theodidactus* proclaiming the prophane
vulgar to depart, of these goddesses you may
read at Large in our *Temple* of *Wisdome*; in
*Esdras* we read this precept concerning the
Cabalisticall secret of the Hebrews declared
in these verses, thou shalt deliver those
Books to the wisemen of the people, whose
hearts thou knowest can comprehend them
and keep those secrets, in the *Temple* of *Wis-*
*dome* you see obscure Figures of Astromancy
and

and Geomancy, whereunto is added the Alphabet of Angels or writing and Language of Haeven, affording compendious words partly by Starrs, Characters set in manner of a wheel thick, the reading thereby being defended from the Curiosity of the prophane therefore my worthy Schollers in this science be silent, and hide those things which are secret in Religion, for the promise of silence is due to Religion as *Tertullian* affirms but they which do otherwise are in great danger, Now concerning these secrets my Ingenious disciples, I would tell you, if it were lawfull to tell you, you should know all, if it were lawfull to hear it; but both eares and tongue would contract the same guilt of rash curiosity, the divine Goddess

( *of God*

*Hester Heaton sings in those verses the power*
*The Heavens Ioves Roiall Pallace, he's King*
*Fountain vertue and God of every thing,*
*He is omnipotent, and in his brest*
*Earth, water, fire, and aire do take their rest;*
*Both night and day, true wisdome with sweet*
( *Love*
*Are all contein'd in this vast bulke of Iove*
*His neck and glorious head if you would see*
*Behold the Heavens high, and Majesty*

*The*

_The glorious Raies of Stars do represent_
_His golden lock, and's head adornament._
And again she sings else where to her
friend _Eugenius Theodidactus_,
_Bright Phebus and the Moon, are the two eyes_
_Of this great Jove by which all things, he_
(_spies_

_His head which predicts all, is plac'd i'th sky_
_From which no Noyse can whisper secretly_
_It pierceth all; his body vast extends_
_Both far and wide, and knows no bounds_
( _nor ends_

_The spatious Air's his breath, his wings the wind_
_By which he flyes far swifter then the mind_
_His belly is our Mother Earth, who swells_
_Into huge Mountains, whom the Ocean fills_
_And Circles, his feet are the rocks and stones_
_Which of this globe are the foundations_
_This Jove under the Earth conceals all things_
_And from the depth into the light them brings._

This goddess commands secresie, and
_Theodorus_ the Tragick Poet, when he
would have reforced something of the misteries of the _Jews_ Scripture to the abhored
actions and deeds of harlots and villains
uppon the stage was deprived of sight,
and the Journimen Traitors or Tailors in
their nativities, Almanacks, and monthly
C _predictions_

Predictions verses and obfervations againft their Sacred Majeftyes King *Charles* the firft and fecond and the *Duke* of *Buckinham* are now deprived of truth, and they cannot write or predict any thing againft this Divine government; but lies & my difciples concurred the difpleafure of *Beata Pulchra* and *Hefter Heaton*, becaufe they interpreted the *phænomæna* of Nature, from the *Harmony* of the *World*, The *Temple* of *Wifdome*, and the *Holy Guide* & publifhed them, they dreamed next that the goddeffes *Hefter Heatan* and *Beata Pulchra* ftood in whores habits before the Brothell houfe and they wrathfully anfwered their admiration, that they were by them violently drawn from their modefty & proftituted every where to all common, by which they are admonifhedthat the cerimonies of the Gods ought not to be divulged, *Pithagoras Socrates Plato Ariftoxenus* kept the Mifteries of God and nature inviolable, but *Plotinus* as *Porphiry* relates, broke the oath whichhe made to his Maftera *Ammonius*, and publifhed his Mifteries, for the punifhment of his tranfgreffion he was burnt with lightning, and confumed alive to his bones with Lice, our Saviour *Chrift* alfo himfelfe while he lived on Earth, fpoke after that manner and fafhion, that only the more intimate Apoftles fhould underftand the

miftery

miftery of the word of God, but the other fhould perceive the Parables only: Commanding moreover that holy things fhould not be given to dogs, nor pearly caft to fwine, I would alfo warn you Readers of the *Harmony* of the *World*, The *Temple* of *Wifome* and the *Holy Guide*, that even as the Divine powers deteft publique things and profane, and love fecrecy: So every *Rofie Cruican* experiment fleeth the publique, feeks to be hid, is ftrengthened by filence but is deftroyed by publication, neither doth any compleat effect follow after all thefe things fuffer lofs, when they are powred into prating; and incredulous mindes; therefore it behoveth a Phylofopher, if he would get fruit from this Art, to be fecret, and to manifeft to none, neither his work nor place, nor time, neither his defire nor will unlefs either to a Mafter or partner or Compaion, who ought alfo to be faithfull beleiving filent, and Digified by nature and education: Seeing that even the prating of a companion, his incredulity and unworthinefs hindreth and difturbeth the effect of every operation, we have now delivered this *Harmony* of the *world*, The *Temple* of *Wifdome* and the *Holy Guide*, in fuch a manner, that it may not be hid from the prudent and intelligent, and yet may not admit wicked and incredulous men

to the Misteries of the *Rosie Crucian*
Philosophy: but leave them destitute and
astonished, in the shade of ignorance and
desperation, you therefore sons of wisdome
and Learning search diligently in the
*Harmony* of the *world*, The *Temple* of
*Wisdome* and the *Holy Guid*, gathering
together our disperfed intentions, which
in divers places we have propounded and
what is hid in one place, we make manifest
in another, that it may appear to you
wise men; For, for you only have we
written, whose mind is not corrupted but
regulated according to the right order
of living, unmarryed, who in Chastity and
honesty, and in found faith fear and reve-
rence of God : whose hands are free from
sin and wickedness, whose manners are
gentle, sober, and Modest, you only shall
find out this knowledge conteined in the
*Harmony* of the *World*, The *Temple* of
*Wisdome* and the *Holy Guide*, which is preserved for you, and the secrets which are
hid by many enigmas cannot be perceived
but by wise men, which when you shall
obtain the whole science of the invincible
*Rosie Crucian* discipline will insinuate it
self unto you and these vertues will appear to you, which the *Rosie Crucians*,
who

who wrought miracles, obtained, but yee
envious Tailors or unworthy Scorpionitts,
Calumniators, sons of base ignorance,
Journimen Traitors, foolish writers of Almanacks and other leudness, that deceives
them that trust him, railing down right
and with studied lyes disparages our
person, that was so kind to them as to lend
them ten pound in Gold and had lent them
100 *l.* if we had not found Them of an
ungratefull ill Nature, we scorn to speak
how much our love was to the sending
and giving great gifts, These in requitall
Provoke men to anger, and quarrell, and
pick words to advantage, and if any man
invite them to fight, then begargly coward-
like run to Law, and bring false witnesses
to justifie their deceitfull devices, to get
money And so some of these Astrologicals
live, at this Leud rate being not worthy of
any regard, But saith a poet.

*Since by thy late lost love, I have found out,*
*Thy frindships fam'd like the Common rout;*
*Who prise mens worths at an vnconstant rate*
*Just as they se' them raised or pres'd by fate,*

When we look uppon his naturall parents, Kindred, and relations, and consider
his

his education, we indeed muft give him his
due title *i. e.* a man that by his own in-
duftry and a little inftruction ( of an
Aftrologer and our felf ) hath obtained
knowledge in Aftrology and Geomancy
and can make an Almanack &c. but he is
fo envious fcandalous and malitious againft
others, that it clouds his better parts, The
late years of tirany admitted ftocking wea-
vers Shomakes, Millers Mafons, Carpenters,
Bricklaiers Gunfmiths Porters, Butlers &c.
To write and teach Aftrology and Phifick,
and what a noyfome fpawn of brates, ( as
*Mr. Talbot* calls them) are generated of the
Frothy brains of thefe illegitimate fcriblers,
that went a whoring after the prefs, and
railed againft Monarthy and all men, & cannot yet love one another, we forbid thefe
to come nigh our writings for they are your
enimies and ftand out a precipice, that ye
may ere and fall head long into mifery;
if any therefore through his incredulity or
dulnefs of intellect, doth not obtain his
defire let him not impute the fault of his
Ignorance to us, or fay that we have erred,
or written falfely and lied, but let him accufe
himfelf, who underftandeth not our writings for they are obfcure, and covered
with divers mifteries, by the which it will
                                        eafily

eafily happen, that many may ere and loofe
their fenfe, therefore let no man be angry
with us, for we are envious againft no
man, but have folded up the truth of this
fcience with many Enigmaes, and difper-
fed it in divers places, for we have not
hidden it from the wife but from the wicked and undgodly and have delivered it in
fuch words which neceffarily blind the
foolifh, and eafily may admit the wife to
the underftanding of them thus being willing to teach any ingenuous man form our
Vergin pallace in

Hermenpolis
  May. 3 1664.
                JOHN HEYDON.


                C 4

To the moſt accoplisht Philoſopher and learned Secretary of Nature,
Mr. *John* Heydon on his *Elhavarenna* or *Ha-*
*maguleh Hampaaneah*. The *Harmony of the*
*World*, The *Temple of Wiſdome*, The *Holy*
*Guide*, *Geia Imperialia*, The *Idea of the Law*,
and his other Admirable works written about
17 years ſinſe, that are now Publiſhed.

NOw the wits do ſally, and attempt your guard;
  O' how your buſie brain doth beat & ward;
*Rally and reinforce! rout! and relieve;*
*Double reſerves, and them an onſet give*      ( fire
*Like marſhall'd Thunder back-dwith ſlames of*
*Storms mixt with ſtormes! paſſion with globes of Ire*
*Yet ſo well diſciplin'd that Iudgment ſtill*
*Swai'd, and not raſht Commiſſionated will*
*No; words in you know order, time, and place,*
*The inſtant of a Charge, or when to face*
*When to perſue aduantage and where to halt*
*When to draw of, and where to re-aſtault*
*Such ſure Commands ſtreams from you that 'tis one*
*with you to vaiquiſh as to look uppon*
*So that your ruin'd Foes groveling confeſs*
*Your conqueſts were their ſate and happineſs*
*Nor was it here your buſineſſe to war*
*With forreign Artiſts: But thy Active ſtar*
*Doth courſe a home bred miſt, Aſtrology*
*And ſhew its guilts degrees, wherein a lie*

                                                          How

*How Simple men abuse it and Geomancy*
*I challenge all against 'them can say*
*Sentence expell them, And let your sun*
*An everlasting stage in honor run*
*By that its motion to thee ye of man*
*Wave still in a Compleat a Miridion.*

March 25 th
   1664.
at 10 ♄ A.M

# Sir. Kepple Drue Baronet.

# To the Admirable *Philosopher* and Law-yer Mr. JOHN HEYDON

THis is no *Wanton Gallant* that lies
  *Angling for babies in his Miſtris's eyes,*
    And think there's no heaven like a bale of
Six horſes and a Coach with a device       (dyce.
A caſt of Lacquies, and a Lady · Bird,
An Oath in faſhion and a guilded ſword.
That ſmoak Tobacco with a face in freme
And ſpeak perhaps a line of ſence to th' ſame,
That ſleeps a ſabbaoth over in his bed
And if his Play-books there will ſtoop to read,
Doth kiſs its band, and Congey a-la-mode,
And when the nights approaching bolt abroad;
Unleſs his honour's worſhips rents not come,
So he ſals ſick, and ſwears the Carrier home:
Elſe if his rare devotion ſwell ſo high
To waſt an hour-Glaſs on Divinity,
Tis but to make the Church his Stage, thereby
To blaze the Taylor in his Rebaldry
Aſk but the Parrot when his diſtreſs ſhall fall,
Like an Arm'd man uppon him, where are all,
Thoſe roſe buds of his Youth, thoſe antique toyes,
Wherein he ſported out his pretious dayes;
What comfort he Collects from Hawk or Hound,
Or if amongſt his leoſer hours he found,
One of a thouſand to redeem that time
Pariſh'd, and loſt for ever in his prime.

C2

Or if he dream'd of an eternal bliſs,
And ſwears God damn him he nere thought of this,
But like the Epicure ador'd the day
That ſhin'd roſe up to eat and drink and Play ;
The more ſprightly Element of pure fire
Above that Gallant doth advance this higher.
This Author's Noble great and wiſe
His Soul aloft doth ſoar above the ſkies.
To God himſelf, And whats to come he knows,
So to prevent impendent dangers ſhewes ;
Sure Jove deſcended in a Leaden ſhowre
To get his Perſeus; hence the fatal power,
Of Taylors Almanacks; Planets thus Alli'd
Fear to commit an Art of Parricide.
Go on brave Sir, and let the world Conſeſs,
You are the greater world, and that the Leſs.


Thomas Revell Eſq;

## To his most Honour'd friend Mr. *John Heydon* upon his most Excellent Philosophy.

Here, here is philosophy; here you may read
   How long the world shall live, and when't shall
Oh' how I am rapt when I contemplate thee   ( bleed
And wind my self above all that I see
Pardon great sir for the Astrologicall Crew,
Gain, when made Bankrupt in the scales with you,
The spirit of your lines, infuse a fire;
Like the worlds soul, which makes me thus aspire,
As he who in his Chracter of light
Stil'd Gods shadow, made it fare more bright
By an Eclipse so glorious : light is dim
And a black nothing when Compar'd to him,
So' tis illustrious to be Heydons Fool
And a Iust trophee to be made his spoile
He span's the Heaven and Earth, and things above
And which is more joyn Natures with there Iove,
He' s proof against th' arttilory of verses
Whom neither Bilbo, nor invention peirces
You'r sure inchanted Sir, your double free
From Astrologers and th're squibbed Poetry,
For a new East beyond the Stars I see.
Where Breaks the day of thy Divinity,
He makes me Earth, Now a star and then,
A Spirit : Now a star and Earth Again;
He Crowns my soul with fire and their doth shine,
But like the Rainbow in a cloud of mine,
Who sees this fire without his Mask, his eye
Must need be swallowed by the Light and dye ;

August 4th at
sun set 1663.
                      Charles Potter Esq;

To the moſt accompliſht Philoſo-
pher and learned Secretary of Nature,
Mr. *John Heydon* on his *Elhavareuna* or *Ha-*
*maguleh Hampaaneah*. The *Harmony of the*
*VVorld*, The *Temple of VViſdome*, The *Holy*
*Guide*. The *Idea of the Law*,

M Oſt Learned Sir, *it rather were my part,*
*At diſtance to admire not here inſert*
*Theſe ruſtick lines, which merit cannot raiſe ,*
What Mortal's able to ſet out thy praiſe ?
The Deity's in explicable, ſo are you
*All that you write we muſt confeſs is* true,
*Unleſs vve have Coymæra's in our brain*
*And what we do not know is falſe maintain,*
*We may deny* Rome *is,* Perſia *doth ſtand*
*Say* Euphrates *no River,* Affrica *no Land,*
Though curious you, have from thoſe places come
Whilſt we our *Ignorance do hug at home*
*The world and all therein you know ſo well*
*The great* Caballs of Heaven and knacks of Hell
*That we may ſafely affirm if that you pleaſe*
*You can another world make with much eaſe,*
All that Dame Nature has, you know and more,
For ſhe to make you rich is now grown poor
*All that I fear ; the fates will call you hence*
*Nature depoſe, and place you on her bench*
*Your knowledge is ſo great it may controul,*
*More worlds then one,* And all your wit can rule.

March 16 die ♄ ⊙        Thomas Tillion a Philoſopher by
♄ 40 P M 1664.        fire to th: Duke of Buckingham·

To his Loving Ingenious friend Mr. John
Heydon upon his *Harmony of the World,*
*Temple of VVisdome,* and *Holy Guide &c.*

My Careless Phrase and words that lye Neglected
  This vertue have, that they'l not be suspected
Others may over praise your Book (for vve
The best things often over-rated see)
So what I write will æqui distant lye,
From polisht Wit, and servile Flattery,
Bees from a bruised Ox, says Maro, breed ,
But you draw honey from a * Tatter'd weed
Who borrow'd of you Gold, yet doth complain
Much of poverty, whose empty Brain,        *an envious
Measures the slow-part Planets by the glass  Alman-
And when th' Nativity's done its poor alas  ackMa-
But now the ventricles of your pregnant brain  kers his
Give birth to a brave man issues without pain  deceit-
Seeing your wit's so pure, your phrase so clean  ful eni-
Your sence so weighty that each lines a chain  my ♃
Of Gold 'twixt Jupiter Hismael and the Gods,  in ♉.
Mercury and Mars that are now at odds
Your Book (like a young true born Eagle may
Behold the sun in publick at noon day.

Cotton May 13
  Sh. 30. A. M.
    Di: ♀                 Frederick Talbot Esq;

To his honour'd Friend Mr. *John Heydon* on his most excellent principles of Philosophy, in *The Harmony of the World, The Temple of Wisdom, The Holy Guid, Hamegaleb Hampaaneah, Elhavareuna, Ocia Imperialia* and the *Idea of the Lavv*; all written near 17 years since, and by Gods Providence now printed.

WOuld you those Pillars see (those *Reliques*) have
[*Ruins* of time *and* knowledge]Seth did save,
*From the impetuous Sea,* when *waves were all,*
*And all were waves within these Pages small*;
*You'l find them in their antient* Luſtre *shine,*
*Not counterfeit, but rich and masculine.*
  *Or what* Egyptian Sages *sometime set,*
*In their* Papyrus *books* (*Rowls vaſtly great*)
*VVhilſt* Arts *and* Letters *were no* common things
*But* Preiſts *and* Poets Princes *were and* Kings,
*E're Learning a* Ludibrium *became*
*To the audacious* Rout [*oh hapeleſs shame!*]
*E're* Sacred Page *vulgar* Thumbs *could soil*
*Thence feeding black* Seditions *lamp with oile.*
  *Books* (Monuments *of banish'd winds*)*do live,*
*And* (*if from pure* Minerva's *born*) *survive*
*VVhen titles, trjumphs,* Arches Name, *become*
*Silent ith' ruins of a ruin'd tombe.*
*VVhen* Scipio's, Pompey's, Cæſar's *Lavrels may*
*By long succeſs of waſting years decay,*
*Good* Books (*eternal products of the brain*
*Not onely live but may grow fresh again*

March 26 1664                W. Smith Maſter of Arts
  & ♄ 30 *A M.*                    of *Clare Hall in Cambridge.*

A Catalogue of those things contained in these Bookes ·

## First Book.

## Second Book.

## Third Book.

# THE
# LIFE
## OF
# John Heydon

The Son of
*FRANCIS* and *MARY HEYDON*
Now of *Sidmouth* in *Devonshire*.

*Ohn Heydon* is not basely but
Nobly descended, The An-
tiquaries derive them from
*Julius Heydon* the King of
*Hungary* and *Westphalia*,
that were descended from
that noble family of *Cæsar Heydon* in *Rome*,
and since in this Royal Race the line run
down to the Honorable Sr. *Christopher
Heydon* of *Heydon* near *Northwich* Sr. *John
Heydon* late Lord Lieutenant of the Kings
*Tower* of *London*, and the noble *Chandlers*
in *Worcester-shire* of the Mothers side

A                              whic 1

which line fpread by Marriage into *De-vonfhire*, among the *Collin's, Ducks, Drues* and *Bears*, he had one Sifter named *Anne Heydon*, who dyed two years fince, his Father and Mother being yet living : He was born at his Fathers Houfe in *Green-Arbour London*, and Baptized at St. *Sepulchres* and fo was his Sifter, and both in the fifth and feventh years of the Reign of King *Charles* the Firft, he was educated in *Warwickfhire* among his mothers' friends, and fo careful were they to keep him and his fifter from danger and to their Books, that they had one continually to wait upon them, both to the School and at home.

He was Commended by Mr. *John Dennis* his Tutor in *Tardebick*, to Mr. *George Linacre* Prieft of *Coughton*, where he learned the Latine and Greek tongues, the War at this time began to moleft the Univerfities of this Nation, He was then Articled to Mr. *Mic. Petley* an Atturney of *Cliffords* Inne with eighty pound, that at five years end he fhould be fworn before Chief Juftice *Bell*, now being very young he apply-ed his minde to Learning, and by his happy wit obtained great knowledge in all Arts and Sciences, afterwards alfo he followed the Armies of the King, and for his valour

Comman-

Commanded in the Troops, when he was by these means famous for Learning and Arms, he Travelled into *Spain, Italy, Arabia, Ægypt* and *Persia,* and gave his minde to writing, and Composed about 20 years since The *Harmony of the World* in two Books, The *Temple of Wisdome* in three Book, The *Holy Guide* in six Books, *Elhavareuna* in one Book, *Hampaneah Hammeguleh* in one Book, *Ocia Imperialia* in one Book, The *Idea of the Law,* The *Idea of Government,* The *Idea of Tyranny* in three parts, The *Fundamental Elements of Morral Phylosophy, Policy, Government and War, &c.*

These Books were written near 20 years since, and preserved by the good hand of God in the Custody of Mr. *Thomas Heydon,* Sr. *John Hanmer,* Sr. *Ralph Freman,* and Sr. *Richard Temple* during the Tyrants time, first one had the Books, then another, &c. And at last at the Command of these Honourable Learned, and valiant Knights they were Printed.

He wrote many excellent things, and performed many rare experiments in the Arts of Astromancy and Geomancy &c. but especially eighty one, the first upon the Kings Death, Predicted in *Arabia* by him to his Friends, The second upon the losses of

A 2                          the

the King at *Worcester* Predicted at *Thauris* in *Persia*, the third Predicted the Death of *Oliver Cromwell* in *Lambeth* house to many Persons of Honour mentioned in hisBooks, the fourth he wrote of the overthrow of *Lambert*, and of the Duke of *Albymarle* his bringing again of the King to his happy Countries, and gave it to Major *Christopher Birkenhead* a Goldsmith at the Anchor by *Fetter lane* end in *Holborn*, the fifth precaution or Prediction he gave to hisHighnefs the Duke of *Buckingham* two Moneths before the evil was practised: And his Enemy *Abraham Goodman* lies now in the Tower for attem ting the death of that Noble Prince. The sixth for Count *Gramont* when he was banished into *England* by the King of *France*, and he predicted by the Art of Aftromancy and Geomancy the Kings receiving of him again into favor and of his marriage to the Lady *Hamelton*. The seventh forDuke*Minulaus* a Peer of*Germany* that the Emperour sent to him, when the Turk had an Army againfthim, and of the death of the Pope the rest are in his Books, And therefore by thefe Monuments the name of *Heydon* for his variety of Learning was famous not onely in *England*, but alfo in many otherNations into which his Books are Translated. And it seems something difficult to determine, whether the sophistication of truth, or the fucus of errors hath of late years been the more Epidemical cheat in Print, it being sufficiently netorious how this generation of Taylors Almanacks, the under-witg a whoring after the Press, and what a noysome spawn of Brats are generated of the froth of illegitemate Brains, not less numerous then spurious, that neither their male content Parents nor Religion, Law, Reason, nor Charity are able to maintain. And although Mr. *John Heydon*'s works be of a more generous extraction, yet they are very far from Complementing themselves with the least vain hopes of exemption from those censures which are common to all men, It is worth an Asterisk to observe how, infeazable it hath been in all ages for the most innocent to escape this Correctio , Divine *Plato* that Prince of Phylofophers is accused for being too confused and immethodical, *Virgil* by some is counted but a shallow and weak witted Poet, and by others charged as if he were wholy beholding to *Homer* for his works, and *Homer* himself is derided by *Horace*, as if he were too drowsie a Poet, *Demosthenes* could not please *Marcus*

*Tullius* in all things, *Trogas Pompeius* doth accuse *Titus Livius* his Orations of fictions and falsities, *Seneca* was Nic-named and called Lime without Sand ; *Pliny* is compared to a turbulent River that taste of many things but digests few, *Hermes* is called by some the dark King, some affirme *Zoroafter* had no depth of Judgement.

An Astrologicall Taylor accuses *Cornelius Agrippa* Kt. *John Heydon*, *Appolonius*, and *Tritemius* of inventing new and strange principles in Phylosophy D. *Brown* is reproved for inconstancy and instability of Judgement: And Mr. *Moor* and *Eugenius Philalethes* for their too much subtilty in some things, Mr. *Hobs* is thought too full of Reason in his Religion, and the Lord *Verulam* is taxed for the length of Learning, *Paracelsus* is envyed for hard words, Sir *Kenelm Digby* is censured by *Tho. Vaughan* Dr. *Barlow* for his tedious distinctions, *Des Cartes* for the perplexity of his Method, and in a word these very learned and most excellent Philosophers Phisitions and Divines that by the profoundness of their Judgement and splendor of their Eloquence have so illustrated the three Kingdomes as that they have left the world Just cause of their Admiration, no hopes of Imitations even those these have not escaped the like Misreprehensions for in the late years, invectives have been written against these men, yet who more learned then Sir *Kenelme Digby*, more eloquent then Dr *Barlow*, who more witty then Mr. *More* and *Eugenius Philalethes*, who more acute then Mr. *Hobs* who more free and flued then Lord *Verulam*, who more delightful and satisfactory then *Gregory* and *Gaffercll*, who more profound in Philosophy then *Henry Agrippa* Knight, who more Candid and ingenious then *Roger L'Estrange*, who more clear and transparent then *Paracelsus*, who more distinct then *Vincent Wing*, and succinct then Dr. *Wallis* yet all these in their respective and incomperable works have met with the said undue reprehensions. If his works therefore shall chance to meet with some waspish humours, let him consider the Climate, Nor is it more then wants a president, or less then needs a Charitable Construction; which is the worst revenge can possibly be executed by such as chuse rather to suffer then offend Mr. *JOHN HEYDON*, For the Taylors amongst the Almanack Makers carp at all the rest and envie all, amongst Philosophers, *Democretus* laugheth at all things *Heraclitus* weepeth at all things *Pyrhius*

things, This *John Heydon*, fears none, con-
temneth none, is ignorant of none, rejoyceth
in none, grieves at none, laughes at none is
angry with none, but being himself a Philosopher he hath taught the way to happiness
the way to long life, the way to health, the
way to wane young being old, and the way
to resolve all manner of Questions, Present
and to Come; by the Rules of Astromancy
and Geomancy, and how to raise the dead.

He is a man of Midle stature tending to
tallness, a handsome streight body an
Ovall ruddy face mixed with a clear white,
his hair of a dark flaxen brown colour soft
and curling in rings gently at the ends of the
Locks, his hands & fingers long and slender,
his leggs and feet well proportioned, so that
to look upon he is a very compleat Gentleman; But he never yet cast affection on a
woman, nor do I find him inclined to marry, He is very often in great Ladies' cham-
bers, and I believe his modest behaviour
ther makes them the more delighted in
his company, The Princes and Peers not on-
ly of *England*, but of *Spain*, *Italy*, *France* and
*Germany*, send dayly to him, And upon e-
very occasion he sheweth strong parts, and

a vigorous brain, his wishes and aimes, and what he pointeth at, speak him owner of a noble and generous heart, this Gentlemans Excellent Books are admired by the world of Lettered men, as the prodigie of these later times(indeed his works before mentioned (if I am able to Judge any thing) are full of the profoundest learning I ever met withall : And I believe; who hath well read and digested them, will perswade himself, there is no truth so abstruse, nor hitherto conceived out of our reach, But mans wit may raise Engines to scale and conquer. I assure my self he is owner of a solid head, and of a strong generous heart, And if any should question my Judgement, they may read the Comendations of both the Universities, *Oxford* and *Cambridge*, besides the learned *Thomas White* and *Thomas Revell*, Esq; both famous in *Rome* and other parts beyond Sea, that have highly honoured this Gentleman in their Books; yet he hath suffered many Misfortunes, his Father was sequestered, Imprisoned, and lost two thousand pounds by *Cromwell*, this *Oliver* imprisoned this son also two year & half or thereabout in *Lambeth*-House : For he and his Fathers Family were always for the King, And endeavoured to the utmost his restoration,

ſtoration, And indeed the Tyrant was cruel to him, but *John Thurloe* his Secretary was kind to him, and pittied his curious youth, And *Joſhua Leadbeater* the Meſſenger kept him ( At his requeſt and Mr. *John Bradley's*) at his own houſe, And gave him often leave to go abroad , but being yet zealous and active for the King, he was again taken and clapt up in *Lambeth*-Houſe, in theſe misfortunes it coſt him 1000 *l.* and upwards, after this ſome envious villains forged Actions of debt againſt him , and put him in priſon, It ſeems at the begining of theſe misfortunes, a certain Harlot would have him to marry her, but denying her ſuit or that he ever promiſed any ſuch thing, and that he never ſpake to her in his life good or evil, She deviſed with her confederates abundance of miſchief againſt him : ſee him ſhe did in ſome Gentlemens company. Many courted him to Marry but he denyed, now there was left(amongſt a few old Almanacks , and ſcraps of other mens wit ) Collected and bequeathed unto the world by *Nic. Culpe* (as his own admired experience) *Alice Culpeper* his widdow, ſhe hearing of this Gentleman that he was an Heir, to a great fortune Courts him by letters of Love, to no purpoſe, 'pofe, the next Saint in order was fhe that calls her felf the *German Princefs*. But he flies high and fcorns fuch fowl, great beafts the firft of thefe two bleffed birds in her life time caufed one *Heath* to Arreft him, & another after him laid Actions againft him, that he never knew nor heard of.

In this perplexity was he imprifoned two years, for they did defire nothing but to get money, or deftroy him, for fear if ever he got his liberty he might then punifh them, He being of a Noble Nature forgave them all their malice and devices againft him, and fcorns to revenge himfelf upon fuch pittiful things, God indeed hath done him the juftice, for this *Heath* Confumes to worfe then nothing, and indeed if I can Judge or predict any thing ) his Baudy-houfes will be Pawned and he will dye a miferable difeafed beggar. His Miftris when he was very young and a Clerke defired him to lye with her, but he like *Jofeph* refufing, fhe hated him all her life, God preferved him from their malice, although one of thefe 3 lewd women fwore this Gentleman practifed the Art Magick, fhe told *Oliver Cromwell*, fhe faw familiar Spirits come and go to him in the fhape of Conies, and her maid fwore fhe had often feen them in his Chamber

Chamber when he was abroad, and sometimes walking upon the house top in a Moon shine night, and sometimes to vanish away into a wall or Aire, and yet she never saw him in her life, nor could she tell what manner of man he was. But these stories were not Credited, and for all these and many more afflictions and false accusations, I never saw him angry, nor did he ever Arrest or imprison any man or woman in all his life yet no clyent of his was ever damnifyed in his suit.

He was falsly accused but lately of writing a Seditious Book and imprisoned in a Messengers Custody. But his Noble friend the Duke of *Buckingham*, finding him innocent and alwaies for the King he was then discharged, and indeed this glorious Duke is a very good and just Judge : and although some speak slightly of him, he studies the way to preserve his King and Countrey in peace plenty and prosperity, it is pitty the King hath no more such brave men as he, a thousand such wise Dukes as this (like Marshal'd Thunder, back'd with flames of fire) would make all the enemies of the King and Christendome Quake; and the Turke flie before such great Generals, in all submission we humbly

bly pray for this Great Prince, and leave him to his pleasure & return to our subject.

*John Heydon* is not of that vain and presumptuous Nature as the Taylors that despise all Artists even *Agrippa, Appolonius, More, Vaughan* and *Tritemius.* And yet they cannot read these and many other Learned Authors they so impudently abuse, Rob of their Learning, and convert other mens parts to their own profit, He lent one Ten pound in Gold, he in requital or return speaks ill of him, and pretends to know many admirable Rules of Geomancy and impertinently addes them to Nativities, and applyes them to all manner of Questions in Astromancy, but his Books being written so long since, *viz.* near twenty years by himself, their greediness of great maters is discovered, and we now know them to be neither Scholers nor Gentlemen, these hang up clouts with here are. Nativities Calculated, Questions resolved, and all the parts of Astrology taught by us----For three pence, four pence, six pence, or higher if you please, thus are young Apprentices, old women and wenches abused and that they may be found, for money, they tell us the 12 Houses of heaven in the sign of a Coat of Arms are

to

to be let, when they might indeed fet bills
upon their brazen foreheads, engraven thus,
*Here are Rooms to be let unfurnifhed,* but
our Author regards not thefe men, all their
fcandals forgeries & villanous devices they
contrive againft him, he flights and fcorns
& hath purpofely forfaken *Spittle-Fields* &
his lodgings there to live a private Life, free
from the concourfe of multitudes of people
that daily followed after him, but if any defire to be advifed let them by way of letter
leave their bufinefs at his Book-fellers, and
they fhall have anfwer & Counfel without
reward, for he is neither envious nor ene-
mie to any man, what I write is upon my
own knowledge.

He writes now from *Hermenpolis* a place I
was never at, It feems by the word to be the
City of Mercury, and truly he hath been in
many ftrang places, among the *RofieCrucians*
And at their Caftles, Holy-houfes Temples,
Sepulchres, Sacrifices, all the world knows
this Gentleman ftudys honourable & boneft
things, and faithfully comunicates them to
others, yet if any traduce him hereafter they
muft not expect his Vindication, he hath re-
fered his quarel to the God of Nature, it is
involved in the concernments of his Truths
and he is fatisfied with the peace of a good
cons

confcience, he hath been mifinterpreted in
his writing, with ftudied Calumnies they
difparage his perfon whom they never faw
nor perhaps will fee, he is refolved for the
future to fuffer, for he fays, *God condemns
no man, for his patience,* the world indeed
may think the truth overthrown, becaufe
fhe is attended with his peace for in the
Judgement of moft men, where there is no
noife, there is no victory, this he looks
upon as no diffadvantage the eftimate of
fuch cenfures will but lighten the fcales,
and I dare fuppofe them very weak
brains, who conceives the truth finks becaufe it outweighs them, as for tempeftious
out-crys when they want their Motives they
difcover an irreligious fpirit, one that hath
more of the *Hurry-cano* then of Chrift Jefus
God was not in the wind that rent the rocks
in peices, nor in the Earth-quake and fire at
*Horeb.* He was in *Aura tenui,* in the ftil fmal
voice, his enemies are forc'd to praife his vertue and his friends are forry he hath not
10000 pounds a year, he doth not refent the
common fpleen, who writes the truth of God
hath the fame Patron with the truth it felf,
and when the world fhall fubmit to the ge-
neral Tribunal, he will find his Advocate
where they fhall find their Judge, there is
mutual

Mutual Teſtimony between God and his Servants, or nature and her Secretary, If the Baptiſt did bear witneſs of Chriſt, Chriſt did alſo as much for the Baptiſt; He was a burning and a ſhining light, when I writ this Gentlemans life God can bear me witneſs it was unknown to him and for no private ends, but I was forc'd to it by a ſtrong Admiration of the Miſtery and Majeſty of Nature written by this Servant of God and Secretary of Nature, I began his Life ſome years ſince, and do ſet it down as I do finde it, if any man oppoſe this, I ſhall anſwer, if you are for peace, peace be with you, if you are for War, I have been ſo too, (Mr. *Heydon* doth reſolve never to draw Sword again in *England*, except the King command him.) Now let not him that puts on the Armour boaſt like him that puts it off: *Gaudet patientia duris* is his Motto, and thus I preſent my ſelf a friend to All Artiſts, and enemy to no man.

*Frederick Talbot* Eſq,

*March* 3
1 6 6 ²⁄₃,

## The Rosie Crucian

# CROWN

Set with Angels, Planets and Mettals &c.

### The First Book.

## CHAP. I.

1 *Of the Gold Mercury or Argent vive.*
2 *Purification.* 3 *Sublimation.* 4 *Cal-*
*cination.* 5 *Exuberation.* 6 *Solution.*
7 *Separation.* 8 *Conjunction.* 9 *Putre-*
*faction into Sulphur.* 10 *Fermentation.*
11 *Multiplication in vertue.* 12 *Mul-*
*tiplication in quantity.*

He that can make the Stone of Argent vive or ☿ alone, is the
greatest searcher out of Art and
Nature : because there is all that
in ☿ which wise men do seek,
for, Quick-silver is the mother
and sperm of all Metals and their nearest matter :
and it is not onely a spirit but a body, it is also

D     2

a middle Nature and also a sulphur, it is a lingring ☿, it dieth and riseth again and is fixed with
its own proper Elements: wherefore it is first necessary that it be purged from its impurities.

The purgation or purification is on this wise;
grind it upon a Marble with a muller or a wodden Pestill in a wodden Morter with common salt
and a little vinegar springled thereupon till the
salt be black, then wash it well with vineger
and dry it easily at the fire, or at the
Sun, then strain it through a double cloath or a
new skin of a sheep till it be dry and the vineger clear taken away and be of a white colour and clear.

Grind it upon a Marble with a little ☿ sublimate and let it mortifie and in corporate
with it: then grind it with its equall weight
of salt-Peter and green Coperas till it be like a
paste: Then put all into a subliming glass
and in Ashes sublime all the ☿ that it be white
and clear as snow in the head of the l imbeck
sublime it again three times or oftener and it
will be pure ☿ and sublimate.

Put one pound of this ☿ sublimate into
two pound of common *Aqua fortis* by little and
little at once as by two at a time till all be
dissolved like sugar in wine then shut the glass
and set it in Balneo to dissolve the space of 10
days then distil away the *Aqua fortis* in a lentheat
in Balneo and the ☿ will remain in the bottome
like butter of a white colour. And calcined by
corrosive water.

Put this calcined ☿ into an Earthen body
with

with a Limbeck and in ashes sublime the whole
dissolved substance three times which will then
be very white and then it is called *Mercury Ex-
uberate.*

VVhen you have three or four pound of this,
receive the third part and fix it by often sublimation till it remain in a hard mass and ascend no
more but remain fixed.

VVhich is called the Glue of the Eagle or the
prepared body permanent and the volatile made
fixed which is to be reserved for the earth of the
stone.

Dissolve the other two parts in Balneo or in a
cold Cellar or put it in a blader and hang it over
fuming hot water till it be allcome to water.

Take this water thus made, and digest it in
a Circulatory well closed the space of nine days
then put it in a body with a head and receiver
well luted and in ashes or *Balneo* distill the water of a white coulour or milkie and is called
*Lac Virginis,* dissolving all mettalls and so you
have seperated the spirit of the stone which is
also called the lingring spirit and the white
Tincture of the white stone of *Mercury.*

Take the third part which before you reserved and fixed called the glue of the Eagle, as
much of it as you please and add thereto equal
weight of its spirit or *Lac Virginis* and close
up the glass and so you have joined the Man
and the woman, ☿ with his own Earth; the
spirit with the body. See the *Holy Guid.*

Set your *Lac Virginis* thus joyned with his
own, Each in *Balneo* to putrifie 150 days and

there

there let it stand unmoved ; after forty days it will be black, and it is then called the head of the Crow : then it will be of a green colour after that the Peacocks tail, and many false colours for between this and white it will appear red but at last you shall see it white and then encrease your fire and it will stick to the sides of the glasse like fishes eyes Then have you each in the nature of Sulpher, *Read the Holy Guid.*

Take of this Sulphur as much as you please and weigh it and add thereto two parts of the white *Tincture* or *Lac Virginis* and set it in Balneo to dissolve the space of six days then distill away the *Lac Virginis* or *Tincture* and the Sulphur will remain in the form of Liquor for it is the liquor of the white sulphur of ☿ which is to be joined with the Liquor of the sulphur of *Luna* or silver.

The Sulphur of the white *Luminary* or silver or *Luna* is made as the other whereof we shall speak more in the next Branch. This Liquor of the sulphur is the soul which is joined with the spirit and body which quickeneth the whole stone. The other conjunction before was onely the union of the spirit and the body : but this is a threefold copulation *viz.* The uniting of the soul, spirit, and body.

Adde equal weight of these two Liquors of sulphur that is to say the liquor of the sulphur of *Mercury* and of silver and *Luna*, and close well the glasse and set it in Ashes till it be white, for it will be of all coulours again and

and at laft white; And then is it the perfect ftone converting all Mettalls into filver.

This ftone or Elixir is thus multiplied in vertue diffolve it in your *Lac Virginis* and diftill it away and dry it and diffolve it again &c. And let it be fo often diffolved and dryed till it will drie no more but remain in an incombuftible oyl. And is then Elixer of the third Order.

Take one part of this Elixir and project it upon 100 or 1000 parts of melted filver (according to the goodnefs and vertue thereof) and it will turn the filver into a brittle Mafs or fubftance, which beat to powder in an Iron or braffe Morter or upon a Marble, and project one part of this powder upon 100 parts of purged made hot, and it will be perfect medicine whereof one part turneth 100 or 1000 parts of other bodies into good filver. And this way is your Medicine multiplyed in quantity.

## A Corollary.

IT remaineth now that we speak of the Medicine or the Elixir of Life, which is called potable silver. But although the Liquor of silver may be made potable silver if it be corroberated before by digestion in Balneo 7 days with the spirit of wine and then distill away the said spirit of wine that the oyl of the silver may remain in the bottome which may easily be given for medicine, Yet the Philosophers would have us do otherwise for they teach us to bring the mettalls first into their quintessence before they be taken inwardly, and that their is no other quintessences but those that are of a second nature according to the old saying,

*Elixir de te est res secunda*
*De quo sunt facta corpora munda.*

That is to say the 4 Elements are destroyed and by putrifaction a new body created and made into a stone, which is the quintessence as *Ripley* would have it ; But I do boldly and constantly affirm that there is no true silver or potable silver nor Qintessence unless it be first Elixir and that is done in a quarter of an hour by projection of the Elixir upon silver or pure gold molten according as the Elixir was red or white. If therefore yon desire after
the

the first composition of the Elixir to make
the *Arcanum* of *Argentum* or *Aurum potabile* project the Elixir or Medicine according
to his quality or property upon pure silver or
gold molten, and then it is made brittle and frangible and grind it to powder and take thereof
so much as you please and dissolve it in distilled vinegar (or rather in spirit of wine) the
space of nine days, then distill away the vineger
or spirit of wine, that which remaineth in the
bottome is the true Medicine, Quintessence,
Elixir of life, Ferment of ferments and incombustible oyl converting mettalls and Mans body
into perfect health from all diseases of mans
body which proceed from *Mercury* and *Luna.*
And thus is the true potable silver made cureing the *Vertigo, Sincope, Spilepsy, Madness, Phrency Leprosie. &c.* And this is the right way of
making the stone of *Mercury* alone : but the
Elixir cannot be made without the Addition
of silver to the white, and of gold to the red.

CHAP.

## CHAP. II.

1 *Luna.*   2 *pure Silver.*   3 *Calcination.*
4 *Solution.* 5 *Putrefaction.* 6 *The Sulphur.*
7 *The Liquor of the Sulphur.* 8 *White Ferment.*

HERMES faith, The Elixir is nothing elfe but *Mercury Sol* and *Luna*, by *Mercury* nothing is underftood but the fulphur of nature which is called the true ☿ of the Phylofophers, and that fulphur gotten by putrifaction by the conjunction of the fpirit and of the body of imperfect bodyes or mettals.

By *Sol* is meant gold, by *Luna* filver, both of them are to be joyned to imperfect bodies, that is to fay, white fulphurs and red, whence the fame *Hermes* in his 7 treatife of *Sol* faith there happeneth a conjunction of two bodies and it is neceffary in our Maiftry; And if one of thefe bodies onely were not in our ftone it would never by any means give any *Tincture*, Upon which *Morienus* faith, For the Ferment prepareth the imperfect body and converteth it to its own nature and there is no Ferment but *Sol* and *Luna*, that is, gold and filver. Of which *Refinus Sol* and *Luna* prepared (that is to fay their fulphurs) are the ferments of mettles in colour. See the *Holy Guid.*

But

But this is made more evident by *Raymund* in his Apertory where he saith there is no ferment except *Sol* and *Luna*, for the Ferment of the stone to white is silver and to the red gold, as the Phylosophers do demonstrate because without ferment there doth proceed neither gold nor silver nor any thing else that is of its kind or nature, therefore join the Ferment with its sulphur that it may beget its like, because the Ferment draweth the sulphur to its own colour, and nature also, and weight and found because every like begetteth its like. Because the Ferment even as *Sol* tingeth and changeth his sulphur into a permanent and piercing Medicine, Therefore the Philosopher saith he that knoweth how to tinge sulphur and Mercury with *Sol* and *Luna*, shall attain to the greatest secret. And for this reason it is necessary that *Sol* and *Luna* be the *Tincture* and Ferment thereof. You may read in the *Holy Guide*.

And so also *Arnoldus* in his *Rosary*, There is no body more noble or pure then Sol, or his shaddow that is to say silver without which no tingeing Mercury is generated. He that endeavoureth to give colour without this gold or silver goeth blindly to work like an *Asse* to a Harp, for gold giveth a golden and silver an argentive colour therefore he that knoweth how to tinge ☿ with Sol and Luna cometh or reacheh to the secret which is called white sulphur, the best to silver which when it is made red, will be red sulphur to gold the best.

Take

Take pure *Luna*, that is to say silver that is best which is beaten into leaves and bring it into calx with ☾ And it is then called water silver then is the Luna well prepared for Calcination. See the *Hely Guide.*

When you have your silver thus prepared, take 4 or 6 ounces thereof, and put it in double proportions of *Lac Virginis* mixed with equall quantity of corrasive water to dissolve in an egge glasse. After it hath dissolved so much as it can in the cold, set in Balneo and there let it stand 9 dayes till the whole substance of the silver be dissolved into a green water, then let the Balneo cool and take it out, and put the dissolution into the body and set thereon a head and distill of the water from the matter remaining which is the oyl of the silver Calcined not into a calx but a Liquor, because this *Lac Virginis* if it be mixed or joned with common *Aqua fortis* or alone without it (as it pleaseth the Operator) is so strong that the very Diamond cannot resist it but is dissolved : Therefore this water is called the water of Hell and is the onely miracle of miracles of the World, because it containeth such a fiery nature in it self and propriety of burning of all bodies into Liquor whereas the Elementall fire prevaileth no further then to reduce mettalls into calx or ashes. But to return from whence we digressed I now come to the third operation.

To the end therefore that this liquor or oyl of silver may be more perfectly dissolved and that all the imperfection of adustion may be

*ratio quod ? Lac Virginis ?* taken

taken away, which by the Antients is called the corroberating of the left humidity. Put this Oyl or liquor into another egge glasse like the former power thereupon so much spirit of wine, above it 4 fingers then close well the glasse and set it in balneo to digest 7 or 10 dayes and you shall find the oyl or liquor turned into a thin or rare water oyl: put this water into a still and in balneo draw away the spirit of wine till none of the spirit of wine remain with the silver dissolved. And thus have you your silver prepared for putrifaction.

This Liquor of silver is potable but not the Quintessence put this water into a fit putrifying glasse and seal it up and set it to putrifie in balneo till the time of putrifaction be past which is about 150 days, and when you see the first sign of putrifaction which is called the head of the Crow encrease your fire a little till all colours begin to appear and you see it begin to be white,

When you see it white encrease your fire yet more and it will rise up and stick to the sides of the glasse most transparent like the eyes of fishes which is Sulphur of Nature or salt, or the putrified body of the white Luminary, *viz. Luna,* which yet is not so hard as a body nor so soft as a spirit but of a mean hardness between a spirit, and a body, and is called the Phylosophers *Mercury* and the Kay and mean of joining Tinctures.

But to come to the liquor of the white Luminary, this body being brought into Quintessence

essence is prepared for dissolution like the sulphur of the imperfect body, but whereas that is done by the vertue of the white tincture or *Lac Virginis* I rather do it by vertue of the fire naturall which is the spirit of wine and after the drawing away thereof it remaineth in a Liquor.

Now this liquor of *Luna* dissolved is the Quintessence which then is the liquor of the white *Luminary* and the sole as *Exiradius* saith quickening the whole stone without which it is dead and will neither give form nor colour.

Therefore the fourth part of this liquor of the white *Luminary* is to be joined to three parts of the former liquor of the sulphur of ♀ and after to be kept in a lent fire of Ashes well closed till it passe through all colours and at last come to its former colour of whitenes and so the stone is fermented and turned into the white Elixir.

The Residue of the foresaid dissolved sulphur keep diligently and therewith ferment the white sulpher of other imperfect bodies or stones into Elixirs, which when they are thrice dissolved and again congealed and remain in a liquid substance then they are called incombustible oyles and Elixirs of the third order.

And thus the stone is made of ♀ alone.

A

## A Corrollary.

HAving spoken of the white stone it now resteth that we speak of the making of the red *Elixir,* vvhereof there is two processes the first whereof is from the Radix *i. e.* the long way : the other an accurtation that is much shorter and more excellent, *And* this way the *Elixir* may be made in 80 days and excells all other accurtations neither is there found therein any diminution of the vertue but is a plentifull and perfect fulnels of power and vertue having a'l the properties which the *Elixir* ought to have. The procefs whereof thefe three follow-ing Chapters will plainly shew.

CHAP

## CHAP. III.

IT is not neceffary to fpeak in this place of the urgation of ♀ becaufe we fpoke thereof before.

The fublimation is to be done otherwife then in the former worke for that which is called fublimation here is not done with vitrioll and falt peter but is only the diftillation of the ♀ in an earthen body with a limbeck and that by it felf without any addilament.

When the ♀ is once fublimed in afhes wholly into the head of the limbeck having a retainer joined thereto take off the head and with a fea-ther gather the fublimed matter and you fhall find your ♀ of a black colour having loft his fairnefs and like a duft or powder flicking to his body.

Put it again into the body and fublime it as before and reiterate this work 7 or 9 times un-till you have a fufficient quantity of this pow-der that is to fay a pound or more. And this is the Calcination.

When

When you see your ☿ will ascend no more but remain in the bottome of a black colour and that is dead and brought perfectly into calx let it cool and remove your body into sand till it be turned into a red colour; And this is the perfect precipitation profe without the help of any corrofive water, take a little of this powder upon a hot iron plate if it fume, dry it longer, if not it is well.

Take of this red powder as much as you will diffolve and put thereupon at leaft his double weight of *Lac Virginis* and fet in Balneo till you fee your *Lac Virginis* ftained a yellow or red colour then filter it from its feces and keep it by it felf in a glafs well ftopped and dry the matter that remaineth in *Afhes* and pour thereon new *Lac Virginis* and do as before till you have drawn out all the tincture. And fo your ☿ is diffolved.

Put thefe folutions into a body luting to a head and in balneo diftill away the *Lac Virginis* and the red oyl precipitate will remain which is fixed and needeth no diftillation but is the tinging oyl of red *Mercury* and the red tincture of the red ftone of ☿ and the foul and fpirit of the fame ftone joyned,

Therefore take part of the white Sulphur referved in the firft Table and rubify it in afhes till it be red then imbile it with equal weight of the oyl of the tincture of this red ☿ and fet it to diffolve in Balneo, and when you fee it is diffolved into a liquid fubftance take it out.

Then fet it in afhes or under the fire to fix till

till the matter being dried remain fixed and fusible standing in a mean .heat not over hot which try upon a hot Iron plate and if it fume not it is well, if it do, encrease your fire till it be totally fixed and dry.

If this matter be imbibed again with its oyl till it drink up as much as it will and again dissolved in Balneo and then dried in Ashes, it will shew many colours and lastly appeared. And then it is the stone penetrating and fusible, apt for forme.

Join this imbiled matter (or stone) with the 4th part of the liquor or oyl of the red sulphur of Gold or the red Ferment, and dissolve it in Balneo, and drie it again, and again dissolve it in a glasse hanged in the fume of hot water or Balneum and congeal it again till it stand like honey; Then it is the perfect red Elixir of *Mercury.*

The Multiplication or Augmentation of the vertue and quantity is shewed in the former Chapter.

CHAP.

## CHAP.  IV.

*1 Gold Sol.  2 Purged Gold.  3 Calcination.
4 Solution.  5 Putrifaction.  6 Filius, Solis Cœlestis.  7 Filia Lunæ Cœlestis.*

THe putrifaction or purgation of gold is done as the Goldſmiths uſe to do by melting it with *Antimony* that the gold may remain in the bottome pure and clear from other mettalis which they call *Regulus.*

Take 4 or 5 ounces of this refined gold, leaſ or fileings and diſſolve it in *Lac Virginis*, mixed with equal weight of *Aqua fortis* wherein ſalt Armoniack ſublimed is diſſolved, and when it is diſſolved into a red Liquor or deep yellow then it is well calcined.

The ſolution and putrifaction is done as before you did with ſilver in the preparation of the white Ferment.

When you have your white ſulphur of nature (after putrifaction) ſticking to the ſides of the glaſs, let it cool, and take out your glaſs and ſet it in Aſhes, and encreaſe your fire but not too much leſt your matter vitrifie, and let your aſhes be no hotter then you can hold your hand therein, and ſo let it ſtand till the ſulphur be of a perfect deep red colour, Then have you the red ſulphur of the red *Luminary.*

If you reſolve this red ſulphur in ſpirit of wine or diſtilled Vineger into an oyl it is then the Li-

E                                         quor

quor of the, red *Luminary*, And *Auram potabile* curing all infirmities if the spirit of wine or vinegar be distilled from it; But for this work it were better to dissolve it in our red *Lac Virginis* spoken of in the second Chapter of the second Book; distill away the *Lac* from the sulphur in Ashes, and the sulphur remaining in an oile is the Ferment of all stones to the red. The augmentation of this red Elixir in vertue is with his red Tincture as before in the white Elixir with his white Tincture. The augmentation in quantity is by projection upon the body of gold molten : And that brittle matter of gold upon ☿ and if it be powdered and resolved with spirit of wine in an oyl as was said before of silver then it is the Quintessence of gold, and the great Elixir of life and the spiritual ferment for the transmutation of mettals and for the health of mans body.

The 5 Chapter sheweth the abbreviation of the Red Elixir.

CHAP.

# CHAP. V.

1 *The Liquor of the red sulphur.* 2 *Fermen-*
*tation.*

ALthough *Raymund* writing to King *Robert*
was pleased to say, That every Accurtation
diminisheth the perfection: because Medicines
which are made by accurtation have less effect of
transmutation, which I also ascent to with him
for a truth, if the work be begun from the first
fountain: yet because this work hath its beginning from those things which before were
brought to a perfect degree of perfection, therefore in this there is no diminution of the perfection as the same *Raymund* witnesseth *lib. Mecur.*
pag. 103. saying thus.

Therefore it ought to be declared unto thee,
that if they be both well prepared (and that thou
begin with them) thou wilt do a wonderful work
without any great labour sooner then if thou
should begin with one thing alone; Therefore
my son begin thy work of two things together as
I shewed to thee in the greater stone, when we
spoke of the twofold custody of the actions
which are caused by the bodies and spirits.

By that which is caused by the bodies and
spirits he means nothing else but sulphur, willing
that we should begin with sulphur, to which I
do so well agree that I begin this my accurtation

with

with sulphur alone and I add no other body to this *Elixir* but onely the sulphur of ☿ alone created of his own body and spirit.

Take therefore 2 ounces of the white sulphur that was described in the first Chapter and set it in ashes to rubifie, in 30 days it will be turned into red sulphur.

Which when you have done dissolve that sulphur in the red Tincture of *Mecury* when it is dissolved draw away the Tincture, in the bottom remaineth the Liquor of the sulphur.

To which if you add a due proportion of the liquor of the red *Luminary* it will be perfect Ferment, which if you dissolve and congeal as before is shewed, it is then Elixir of very great vertue to the red work and no man can make a shorter abreviation in the world ; And when the sulphur of any body is prepared it may this way very speedily be converted into Elixir by adding the liquor of the ferment.

CHAP

# CHAP VI.

1 *The Body.* 2 *The Spirit.* 3 *The Lion.* 4 *The Eagle.* 5 *The Phylosophers Lead.* 6 *Antimony.* 7 *Antimony Mercury.* 8 *The Glue of the Eagle.* 9 *Solution of the red Lion into Blood.* 10 *Solution of the Glue of the Eagle.* 11 *Solution of the Blood of the red Lion.* 12 *Conjunction.* 13 *Putrifaction.* 14 *The Stone.* 15 *Fermentation.* 16 *In the Trinity of The Phisical and Alchimical Tincture The Soul.* 17 *Is the Unity of the Medicine.*

TAke Antimony calcined so much as you please, and grind it to a subtile powder, then take twice so much *Lac Virginis* and put your powder of Antimony therein and set it in baineo 7 days, then put it into a body, and set it in sand or ashes till the *Lac* be turned red, which draw of and pour on more and so let it stand, when that is coloured red, pour it to the other and thus do till you have drawn out all the tincture set all this water in balneo or lent ashes to distill with a Limbeck, and distill it with a lent fire and first of all the *Lac* will ascend, then you shall see a stupendious Miracle because you shall see through the nose of the Alimbeck as it were a thousand veins of the liquor of this

blessed

bleſſed minere to deſcend in red drops juſt like bloud, which when you have got thou haſt a thing whereto all the treaſure in the world is not equall; Now you have the blood of the Lion according to *Rupeſiſſa*, let us here reſt a little and ſpeak of the Glew of the Eagle, of which *Paracelſus* thus ſaith.

Reduce Mercury ſo far by ſublimation till it be a ſixed Chriſtall; this is his preparation of Mercury and his way of reducing it into the Glew of the Eagle, but above all I require that that way be uſed which is deſcribed by me before in the firſt Chapter, or that hereafter ſet down after this.

Then ſaith the foreſaid Author, go on to reſolution and coagulation, and I again will you to obſerve the ſame manner of ſolution ſhewed in the firſt Chapter before.

Now let us come to conjunction after the ſolution of theſe two, take equal weight of them and put them in a veſſel well ſhut.

After you have thus joined them together ſet your glaſs in your furnace to putrifie and alter the ſpace of certain days. Therefore *Paracelſus* ſaith, then at length and preſently after your *Lili* is made hot in your glaſs it appeareth in wonderful manners (or demonſtrations) blacker then the Crow: after that in proceſs of time whiter then the Swan and then paſſing by yellow to be more red then bloud.

This being putrified and turned into red is to be taken for the ſtone, and then it is time it be fermented.

Of

Of which Fermentation Paracelsus thus speaketh, one part thereof is to be projected upon 1000 parts of molton gold, and then the medicine is prepared and this is the Fermentation of it. But if the half or one part of the liquor of the sulphur of gold before described be added to it then it would be spirituall ferment, and would be much more penetrating in fortitude and fusible as *Paracelsus* doth testifie in his *Aurora* where he would have us to join the star of the sun or the oyl of sol to this stone. And thus the phisical Alchimical tincture is performed in a short time for curing all manner of Infirmities and humane diseases (which is also the great Elixir for mettals) so courtly concealed by the Antients. Which *Hermes Trifmagiflus* the *Ægyptian, Cfus* the *Gretian, Haly* an *Arabian,* and *Albertus Magnus* a *German,* with many others, have sought and profecuted every one after their own method, and one in one subject another in another, so much defired by the Philosophers onely for prolongation of life.

In this composition *Mercury* is made a fixed and diffolved body, the blood or spirit of the red Lion is the ferment or foul, and so of trinity is made unity, which is called the Phisical and Alchimicall tincture, never before that I knew of collected or writ in one work And I swear: I had not done this except that otherwise the composition of this blessed medecine had for ever been forgot.

### *A shorter way to make the glue of the Eagle.*

If you desire to make the glue of the Eagle in a breifer way. Take part of the red precipitate prole as is taught before in the table of *Mercury* and dissolve it in distilled vineger and the vineger will be coloured into a yelow or delightfull golden colour and after you have destilled away the vineger there will remain in the bottome a white substance of the *Mercury* fixed and fair, which is to be joyned to the oyle of the Lion; And this work is much shorter and less laborious, look more hereof in the third Book.

### *The Calcination of Antimony into the red Lion.*

Take Antimony well ground so much as you please and melt it in naked fire with salt Armoniack, and when it is melted cast it suddainly into a vessel almost full of distilled vineger wherein salt Armoniack hath been dissolved and thus melt it and cast it in three times, then pour off the vineger from the Calx of the Antimony and drie it well and grind it small and dissolve it as before is taught, and so have you the Red Lion of the Philosophers Lead or Antimony.

CHAP.

## CHAP. VII.

1 *Elixir.* 2 *Conjunction.* 3 *Seperation.* 4 *the Stone.* 5 *Fermentation.* 6 *The Earth.* 7 *Spirit oyl, Blood of the Lambe.* 8 *Distillation.* 9 *Resolution.* 10 *Putrifaction.* 11 *Solution.* 12 *Vitrioll.* 13 *Calcination* 14 *Copper.*

# *The first Chapter of the Elixir* of Copper

MAny have fought out the way of the *Mineral* stone in *vitrioll* or green *Copperas,* but they were altogether received which common *vitrioll* by the Philosophers is called the green Lion of fools.    But this our noble red Lion taketh its original from the Metallick body of *Copper.* Although I am not ignorant how to draw an oyl out of *Romain vitrioll* of a more sweet smell and delightsull taste then any balsome if the Tincture be taken out of the calcined *vitrioll* in spirit of wine, yet the Philosophers will is, and command that it do consist of a Metallick vertue wherewith the transmutaion of mettalls is to be effected. Therefore they say it is to be made of bodies and not of spirits as of *vitrioll* sulphur as well and the like. Whence I find it written in the
Philosophers

Philosophers *Turba* and in the first Exercitation :
But the Philosophers stone is a metallick matter
converting the substances and forms of imperfect mettalls, and it is concluded by all the Philosophers that the conversion is not made except by its like, therefore it is necessary that the
Philosophers stone be made of a metallick matter,
yet if any be made of spirits yet it would be
better and much more Philosophical and more
near to a metall ck nature to be made of bodies
then of spirits: but if by Art the body should
be turned into a spirit then the same body
would be both body and spirit, and not to be
doub'ed but the stone might be made of such a
body or spirit. but let us return to our purpose;
It being granted that this our vitriol is such a
body according to which *Paracelsus* testifyeth
in his *Aurora Philosophorum* under this *Ænigura* or secret of the Antient Philosophers.

*Visitabis Interiora Terra Rectificando Invenies
Occultum Lapidem Veram Medicinam.*

Out of the first letter of every word of this
*Ænigura* is gathered this word VITRIOLUM
by which is meant that thereof the stone or medicine may be made.

Therefore *Paracelsus* saith, the inward parts
of the Earth are to be visited ; not onely the
Earth wch is vitriol, but the Inward parts
of the Earth, he meaneth the sweetness and redness, because there lieth hid in the inward parts
of vitriol a subtill noble and fragrant juice and
pure oyle.                                         And

And this is especially to be noted the production of this Copper into vitrioll is not to be done neither by calcination of the fire nor distillation of the matter, lest it be deprived of its greenness which being lost it wants both power and strength.

*Paracelsus* speaks not one word of the preparation of this vitriol by whose silence many have erred, therefore I determined to leave him here a little and to prosecute and follow the order of the Table wherefore I begin with the calcination of the metall. And note that this calcination of Copper is made that it may be turned into vitrioll and not the calcination of vitrioll made of copper.

Take therefore as much copper as you please and dissolve, Calcination it in *Aqua fortis* to a fair green water, then set it 3 or 4 days to digest till the matter be clear which pour out into a limbeck and in Balneo draw away the corrasive water so that the matter remain dry for then it is calcined. .

Then upon every 2 pound of this calcined matter pour a gallon of distilled Vinegar and lute it up in a glass, and set it in balneo almost boyling the space of 7 days, when it is cold put into a limbeck to distill away all the vinegar in balneo, and in the bottom of the Alimbeck you shall have your vitrioll very well congealed far fairer then Romain vitrioll which is corporeal and metallick vitrioll.

Which Vitrioll I do not dissoive in rainwater like the *Paracelsians,* but rather with

L          c

*Lac Virginis* as before is taught in the former Chapters or in *Raymunds* Calcination water, and after its dissolution and perfect digestion, that is to say 15 days I put it into a limbeck and balneo draw off the *Lac virginis,* which being done you shall find an oylie water green and clear upon which pour the spirit of wine and after it hath been digested 7 days and the spirit of wine distilled away in balneo you shall find your green water perfectly rectified made pure subtile and spiritual, and apt for putrifaction, for if it be not well dissolved and rarified it will not putrifie.

But now that I may join with *Paracelsus* in the manner of putrifaction I return to him and say with him commanding to disgest in a warm heat in a glass well closed the space of some moneths, and so long till diverse colours appear and be at length red which sheweth the termination of its putrifaction.

But yet in this process this redness is not sufficiently fixed, but is to be more fully purged from its feces in this manner.

Resolve it or rectifie it in distilled vinegar, till the vinegar be coloured then filler it from its feces. This is its true Tincture and best resolution and rectification out of which a blessed oyl is to be drawn.

This Tincture being thus resolved and rectified, is to be put into a body with a limbeck and in balneo distil the vinegar gently away.

Then

Then in fand or afhes lift up the fpirit gently
and temperately, and when you fee a fume afcend
into the glafs and red drops begin to fall out of
the nofe of the limbeck into the receiver, then
the red oyl beginneth to diftil, continue your diftillation till all be come over, when it is done
you fhall have the oyl in the receiver lifted up
and feparated from its *Earth* more delightful
and fweet then any balfom, or Aromatick without any fharpnefs at all, which oyl is called the
blood of the Lamb. In the bottome of the
body you fhall find a white fhining Earth like
fnow, which keep well from duft and fo you
have the clear Earth feperated from its
oyl.

Take this white Earth and put it in a glafs
viol, and put thereto equal weight of the oyl
or foul and body, will receive it and embrace
it in a moment.

But that it may be turned into a ftone
when you have joined thefe two together, fet
it into our furnace the fpace of 40 days and
you fhall have an abfolute oyl of wonderful
perfection wherewith *Mercury* and other imperfect mettals are turned into gold. As *Paracelfus* was pleafed to fay.

The ftone being thus made, I now come to the
fermentation without which it is not poffible to
give form to it neither will I adhere to the opinion of one man alone contrary to all the Philofophers alone, that is to fay, *Paracelfus* repugnant to the reft of the Philofophers becaufe they
all of neceffity have decreed to give form to the
ftone

ftone by ferment and union, that is to fay, of an imperfect body. and by how much the ferment is more fpirituall the ftone will be of fo much more penetration and tranfmutation.

These things being promifed I do not think it fit that you fhould proceed to projection upon *Mercury* inftead of fermentation as *Paracelfus* teacheth, or that the ftone fhould be fermented his way with gold either corporea l or fpiritual.

Which gold will be the foundation of the firft projection. but what do the Philofophers command us to do? that projection that is to fay fermentation, be made of a perfect foundation, and that upon imperfect bodies that medicines may be made which foundation of the ftone or Elixir is not except it be onely the white or red ferment, in refpect of which both gold and filver are faid to be imperfect bodies, therefore this ftone is to be fermented before it be projected upon the corporeal foundation or imperfect, that is to fay corporeal gold.

Therefore joyn this oyle to the fourth part of the oyle of the fulpur of gold, and this is the true fermentation or converfion unto the Elixir.

Then Augment it in vertue by folution and coagulation, and in quantity by projection firft upon the corporea foundation that is to fay gold, then that upon purified *Mercury* and that medicine upon other bodies which are moft fit for projection, that is to fay moft fufible

a<sub>3</sub>

as Lead or Tinne, which after they are purified are most apt by reason of their easie melting.

And thus the Inward parts of the Earth are
visited and by reflection the hiden stone
is found, the true Medicine out of the
green Lion of the Philosophers, and not
of fools, and out of Corporeal and metallick vitrioll not terrestrial and made of
mineral coperas.

## The Second Chapter of Augmentation and projection of the STONE.

FIRST, Let us speak of the Augmentation
of the vertue or quality; of which *Raymund* saith, The Augmentation in quality and goodness is by solution and coagulation of the Tincture, that is to say, by imbibing
it with our *Mercury* and drying it. But let
us hear *Arnoldus* more attentively, take one
part of your prepared Tincture, and dissolve it
in three parts of our *Mercury*, then put it in
a glass and seal it up and set it in ashes till it
be dry and come to a powder, then open the
glass

glafs and imbibe it again, and dry it again
And the oftener you do the thus fo much fha
you gain and giveth more tincture.

And alfo as it is found in *Clanger Buccine*,
Diffolve it in the water of *Mercury* of which
the Medicine was made till it be clear then congeal it by light decoction and imbibe it with its
oyl upon the fire till it flow by vertue whereof it will be doubled in tincture, with all its
perfections as you will fee in projection becaufe the weight that was before projected upon a thoufand, is now to be projected upon
ten thoufand, and there is no great labour in this
multiplication.

Again the medicine is multiplyed two manner
of ways.

By folution of calidity and folution of vari-
ty. By folution of calidity, is that you take
the Medicine put in a glafs veffel and burie it
in our moift fire feven days or more, till the
medicine be diffolved into water without any
turbulency. By folution of rarity, is that you
take your glafs veffel with your medicine and
hang it in a new brafs pot full of water that boil-
eth and clofe up the mouth of the pot that the
medicine may diffolve in the vapour of the
boiling water.

But note that the boiling water muft not
touch the glafs wherein the medicine is but
hang above it three fingers, and this folution will
be above it in 2 or 3 days after your medicine is
diffolved, take it from the fire to cool fix and
con-

congeal and be hard and dry this do often and
and how much the more the medicine shall be
dissolved it will be so much more perfect, and
such a solution is the sublimation of the medicine and its virtual sublimation, which the oftener it is reiterated so much more abundantly and
more parts it tingeth.

Whence *Rasis* saith the goodness of this multiplication consisteth in the reiteration sublimation and fixation of the medicine and by how
much more this order is repeated it worketh so
much more and is augmented for so often as you
sublime your medicine and dissolve it you shall
gain so much every time in projection one upon a thousand and if the first fall upon a thousand the third upon a hundred thousand the
fourth upon a million and so infinitely. For
*Morienus* the Philosopher saith ; Know for
certain that the oftener our stone is dissolved
and congealed the spirit and soul is joined
more to the body and is retained by it and
in every time the Tincture is multiplyed.

Whence we thus read in *Scala Philosophorum,* which also the Philosophers say. Dissolve
and congeal, so without doubt it is understood
of the solution of the body and soul with the
spirit into water and congealation makes the
soul and spirit mix with the body and if with
one solution and simple congealation the soul
and spirit would be perfectly joined to the
body the Philosophers would not say dissolve
again, and congeal, and again dissolve and congeal that the Tincture of the stone may grow

E.                    if,

if it could be done with one congealation only.

The Medicine is another way multiplyed
by fermentation and the ferment to the white
is pure filver, and the ferment to the red is
pure gold, therefore project one part of your
medicine upon 2 of the ferment (but I fay 3
parts of the medicine upon one of the ferment)
and all will be Medicine, which put in a glafs
upon the fire and fo clofe it that no air go
in nor out, and keep it there till it be fubtili-
ated as you did with the firft medicine and
one part of the fecond medicine will have as
much vertue as one part, of the firft medicine
had (but here again *Clangor Buccine* hath erred
for it fhould be write thus) one part of the
fecond medicine will have as much vertue as
ten parts of the firft medicine had. And thus by
folution and fermentation the medicine may
be multiplied infinitely.

We have fpoken enough of this multiplication, we now come to the other way of augmentation which is called corporeal multiplication and according to *Raymund* is thus de-
fined.

Augmentation is the Addition of Quantity;
whence *Anicen* writeth, It is hard to project
upon a million and to preducate it inconti-
nently wherefore *I* will reveal one great fecret unto you, one part is to be mixed with a
thoufand parts of its neareft in kind ( I call'
that neareft that is the body of the fame mettal whereof the medicine was made or perfected)

perfected) but to return again to *Anicen*, close
all this firmly in a fit vessel and set it in a furnace of fusion 3 days till it be wholly joined
together.   Whereof it is more largely and
better set down by the said Author and
the manner of the work is thus projected, one
part of the foresaid medicine upon 100 parts
of molten gold and it makes it brittle and
will all be medicine whereof one part projected a hundred of any melted mettall converteth it into pure gold and if you project it upon silver in like manner it converteth all bodies
into silver.

In *Scala Philosophorum* all sorts of projection
is set thus down in few words. You must
know that first it is said project, that is to
say one upon 100 &c. yet it is better to project *nunc dimittis* upon *fundamenta* and *fundamenta* upon *verba mea* and *verba mea* upon
*diligans te Domine* and *diligam te* upon *attendite.* This breif *Aenigua* is thus expounded
it is nothing elfe but the words and opinion
of the former Author concealed under the
*Aenigura.* Therefore let us repeat the words
of this *Aenigura* or Oraccle.

> *Nunc dimittis super fundamenta*
> *Fundamenta super verba mea*
> *Verba mea super diligam te*
> *Diligam te super attendite,*

These are trifles for the hiding and concealing the perfection of the Art if the expert Artist could be diverted with such simple words which though they are hard at first to young Artists, yet they are thus explained. We therefore begin with the first sentence.

*Nunc dimittis super fundamenta.*

This is here Allegorically taken for the last action almost of the work which is called the medicine or stone, which medicine is to be projected upon the ferment that is to say upon the oyl of *Sol* or *Luna*, which are the ferments or foundations of the Art in spiritual augmentation (as before was said) upon molten gold and silver. And that spiritual ferment converted into medicine is to be projected upon molten gold or silver which are corporeal ferments in corporeal Augmentation and the corporeal fundaments of the Art upon quick silver.

*Fundamenta super verba mea.*

This is also spoken allegorically because in the *Adage* it is said words are wind, as if a word were nothing else but the motion of the lips and exhaltation of the lungs which no sooner arise from motion but fly away and are turned to air so likewise Quick silver or *Mercury* goeth out of the bodies of other

mettalls

mettalls, and is so volatile in the fire or heat as words in the air. And therefore *Mercury is likened to words* upon which the fundaments are to be projected,

*Verbes mea (vir Mercury) super diligam te.*

That is to say upon other mettalls which have most affinity with quick-silver, and easie of fasion as *Saturn* and *Jupiter* that is to say Lead and Tin, which by this concord and love are easily by the penetration and amiablenefs of the medicine converted into medicine. And one part of this medicine converteth other parts of mettalls into gold or silver according to the force and power of the Elixir, which other mettalls becaufe they are the fubftances of the former bodies whereof the medicines were made. They are the attendants of thofe medicines wherefore the Philofopher commandeth that.

*Diligam te* be projected upon *attendite* that the fecond medicine or this laft projected upon mettal efpecially that whereof the medicine ( that is to fay the ftone) was made, fhould turn that mettall into gold or filver according to the proverty and quality of the medicine.

But to put an end to this projection, take it according to the opinion of *Arnoldus* gathered medicine laft congealed upon 100 parts of *Mercury* wafhed and all will be gold or filver, in all tryalls according as the Elixir is white and red Laftly that I may briefly rehearfe the abfolute manner of projection. Firft the medicine is to be projected upon gold or filver molten, then upon quickfilver purged fo long till it turns it into medicine and laftly upon mettals moft near, that they may be converted into pure gold or filver according to the properties and qualities of the medicine.

Becaufe we have faid fomething of the propinquity of mettalls that is to fay, that the Elixir is to be projected upon that imperfect body out of which its *Mercury* and fulphur was firft extracted, therefore it will not be unneceffary to fet down one example that is to fay if the medicine was made of *Mercury* then it is to be projected upon quick filver for makeing gold or filver becaufe quick filver is a near body to *Mercury* and fo of the reft. Yet it is to be noted, that all Elixirs may and ought to be projected upon quickfilver, becaufe quickfilver is the Mother and fperm of all mettals therefore quick filver made and turned into medicine, is to be projected upon a body, moft near to it; Which is Lead or Tinne; Upon which the medicine is always to be projected, whether white or red for the making and tranfmuting of mettals, but both the quickfilver and lead are firft to be purged that they may be purified and deprived of their filth.

Enough

Enough hath been said before of the purgation or putrification of Mercury. We will
now speak of the putrification of lead.

Melt your Lead in a Crucible and when it
is melted let it stand in the fire a quarter of
an hour and put therein a little salt Armoniack
and let it stand a while in the fire and
stir it with an Iron spatula till all the salt
Armoniack be gone away in fume then scrape
the skin away out of the crusible, that is upon the lead, then let it stand to cool and it
will be much whiter and fairer. And thus you
must purifie your lead or tinne, before projection, because no other bodies are so fusible and apt to melt wherefore every Elixir
ought to be projected upon quicksilver and
upon Lead or Tinne for making or transmuting
of mettals.

But to the end the manner of projection
may be yet more plain I will set down two
rules which must be carefully observed.

The first whereof is that the first medicine
that is to say the stone be projected upon
the ferment always three parts of the medicine upon one of the ferment and one part of
this upon 10 or 100 of pure molten gold, and
one part of this medicine thus made upon
100 parts of an imperfect body, that is to say,
of *Mercury* for medicine. The later is that you
must always consider the fortitude and debili-
ty of your medicine for it is to be projected
so often upon quicksilver as it bringeth it into a brittle medicine and when it faileth then

project

Project one part thereof upon Lead or Tinne for making transmutation, according to the order and form of the Elixir.

These being remembred you may easily conceive the order of Augmentation in vertue and quantity.

These Chapters being ended the other three which follow are set down in the next book, because we have spoken before of potable gold and silver, it is therefore necessary after we have made an end of projection to set down another table of the Elixir of life in the next place, and after speak of its vertue and power as we find it among all the Antient and modern Philosophers and so make an end of the first Book.

*FINIS.*

*Hammeguleh Hampaaneah,*

OR THE

*Rosie Crucian*

# CROWN

SET WITH

Seven Angels, 7 Planets, 7 Genii,
12 Signes, 12 Idea's, 16 Figures, and
their Occult Powers, upon the 7 Mettalls and
Miraculous' vertues in Medicines; with the
perfect full discovery of the *Pantarva* and *Elixirs* of Mettalls prepared to cure the Diseased.

Whereunto is Added

## ELHAVAREUNA

*Presoria, Regio Lucis,* and *Psonthon* Books
much desired by the learned of the world,
Now Compleated and Communicated to all
manner of Persons.

By *John Heydon* Gent Φιλονόμ℮ A Servant of
God and Secretary of Nature.

*London*, Printed by *P. L.* for *Samuel Speed*, and
are to be sold at the *Rain-bow* in *Fleetstreet.*
— 1665.

To the truly honourable and excellently Accomplished the most Renowned,

# John Lloyd Esq.

Externall internall and eternall felicity be wished.

## SIR.

I Dedicate *my Books to you, and your Noble brother because wisdome and vertue cannot be parted, but being my two guards of safty or preserving Patrons to defend me from* envie *and Malice, I presume to call you* Governour of *my* Regio Lucis, *and him* Protector of Elhavareuna, *or the High Preift* of the *Rolie Cross*, and the Harmony of the world, *the* Temple of Wisdome. *The* Holy Guide,

Guide, *Contain the power of Natural sciences and the most absolute Consummation thereof, and that which is the Active part of* Figures *which by the help of the naturall vertues of Mettalls, from a Mutuall and opportune application of them, brings forth opperations even to Admiration, which sciences the* Rosie Crucians *taught when they came to worship our Saviour* Christ *when he was born. The Princes of all places did study these sciences, as* Hiarthas *King of the* Caldeans, Jespion *Prince of the* Brackmans, Phroates *The* Indian Prince, Aftaphon *Duke of the* Gimnsophifts, Budda *King of* Babilon, Numa Pompillius *King of the* Romans Zamoxides *Emperour of* Thrace, Abbaris *Priest of the* Hiperborean Jewes, Hermes Trismegift *a King and Law-* ▒▒▒▒▒▒▒▒▒ Zoroafter *the son of* O- ▒▒▒▒▒▒▒▒▒ Perfia, *All these and many more were Lovers of these* Rofie Crucian *Infallible Axiomata, and both writers and patrons of this Kind of Learning, as* Josephus *The* Hebrew Hermes Eranthes *King of* Arabia &c. *And* ▒▒▒ *to relates in* Alcibiades *that the sons of the* Persian Kings *were instructed in these sciences, that they might Learn to administer, and distribute their Image to the* Common-wealth *of the world, and the* Common wealth *to it : and*

Cicero *saith in his* Books of Divination, *that there was none amongst the* Persians *did enjoy the* Kingdome, *but he that had first Learned* Philosophy, Rosie Crucians *Contemplate the powers of* Naturall, *and* Cœlestial *things, and searching curiously into their* Simpathy *doe produce incredible powers in* Nature *into* Publique *veiw, so Coupling Inferiour* Telesines, Images, Gamahes *and other things as Allurements to the* Gift *of superiour* Angels Planets Genii, Idea's *And* figures *and other things, that by the* Mutuall *application of* Angels Planets and stars *to* Genji and figures *of* Geomancy *upon* Mattalls, *arise wonderfull* Miracles, *not so much by Art as by Nature, to which Art becomes an Assistant whilest it works these things* eelctions being made *of* hours *when* Angels *and* Planets are strong, figures and Characters *rightly engraven or cast uppon prepared* Spermatick pure Mettall *clear and fine, free from any* Mixture. *and all fitted to the* Angel planet signe Idea, *figure of* Geomancy *and these must be applyed to the person of the* Querent *or* Native, *signified by the* Angel Planet signe Genius Idea *and figure, who shall then find the* Cœlestiall *and terrestriall powers, unite to his desire, and performe*

forme incredible extraordinary things, at certain, times Naturally and Roſie Crucians
as the moſt curious ſearchers of Nature.
making uſe of theſe things that are prepared
by Nature only, by appling fiery active
things to Earthly paſſive things, produce
oftentimes effects before the time ordeined
by Nature, which the envious ſcriblers
think are Miracles and cry them down
as Magicall with and in their under opinion
termed Diabolicall, which ineed are Naturall
works; the prevention only of the time
coming betwixt, as if any one ſhould produce Roſes in the Month of March, and apple
trees Blow and bear fruit in December and
Ripe cherries, Grapes and Beans in January
or make parſly grow into perfect plant within
few hours, and cauſe greater things then
theſe, as Clouds, rain, Thunders, and ani-
mails of divers kinds and raiſe the Dead,
And ſpot Horſes black and white like ſtars
or any other colour, and very many tranſ-
mutations of things theſe Books and Arts I
ſubmit ( you excelling in Jugment and Can-
dour ) to your cenſure, that if I have wrote
any thing which may end either to the con-
tumely of Nature, offending God, or injury of
Religion, you may condemn the errour; but
the ſcandall of Malicious perſons being diſ-
                                                    ſolved,

ſolved, you may defend the tradition of Truth, And that you would do ſo with theſe Books, and my ſelf, that nothing may be Concealed which may be profitable, and nothing approved of, which cannot but do hurt, by which means the Harmony of the World, The Temple of Wiſdome, The Holy Guide, Regio Lucis and Elhavareuna, having paſſed your examination (aſwell as my other Patrons) with approbation, may at Length be thought worthy to come forth with good ſucceſs in publique as my otherBooks, and may not be afraid to come under cenſure of poſterity, becauſe I wear the moſt Noble title of.

Aprill the 5 th
at noon
. 1664.

Your moſt affectionate
humble Servant and
true honourer.

## JOHN HEYDON.

The Rofie Crueian

# CROWN

Set with Angels, Planets and Mettals *&c.*

---

*The Second Book.*

---

## CHAP. I.

Of the bleffed ftone of the Philofophers or the Elixir of life, and alfo the way of making malleable glaffe.

1 *Elixir of life.* 2 *Gold diffolved.* 3 *Silver diffolved.* 4 *Gold melted.* 5 *melted Silver.* 6 *Projection of the red Medicine.* 7 *Projection of the white Medicine.*

HERMES Speaking of fermentation bids us to take the fun and his fhadow. by the fhadow he meaneth the moon becaufe in refpect of dignity lufthe and power fhe is much more weak and inferiour then the fun

And

And the moon followeth the sun as a shadow doth the body and is not illuminated except by the light of the sun, we will first speak of the body, that is to say of gold, and after come to the shadow of which gold it is written in a book of Chimicall Art in this manner. The Philosophers stone is made of gold alone and onely by nature and is more sublime then them, which the Philosophers affirme cureth all infirmities. According to the opinion of this Philosopher I purpose to begin with gold alone and the medicine which is a new and sole nature, and antient and found Quintessence.

But to the end this gold may be better and more pure, it may be purged two manner of wayes that is to say, by Antimony and by dissolution in corrosive waters with which copper plates are mixed as Goldsmiths use to do which is called water gold.

When you have thus prepared your gold project one part of your red medicine (or red Elixir) upon 100 parts thereof when your medicine is augmented in vertue and all that weight of molten gold will be converted into a red brittle masse which grind upon a marble to an impalpable powder.

Then dissolve these hundred parts or so much thereof as you please in distilled vineger or in spirit of wine, and set it to disgest in Balneo the space of a day or two then distill the spirit of wine from it in Balneo, and in the bottome will remain the fixed and pure oyl of the gold

G which

which is then the true *Aurum potabile*, and spiritual Elixir of life. If you would give to any one of this powder presently before it be converted to oyl, warm a little white or Rhenish wine and dissolve in either of them so much of the red powder as will tincture the same into a red colour and the wine so tinctured will be *Aurum potabile*, but it would be better and more penetrating if it were tinctured with the foresaid oyl.

In like manner is the white medicine to be projected after the purification of the silver in a corrosive water as is before declared.

And so the melted silver will be converted into a brittle powder and white masse which likewise is to be dissolved and turned into oyl and thus the white Elixir of life is made and potable silver curing and healing so far as it is able humane diseases for it cannot be supposed that the Elixir of *Luna* hath so great vertue as the Elixir of *Sol* hath.

Whence the Author of the book call'd *correctio falnerum* and *Richard Anglicus* in his correctory, say whereas among the vulgar and Philosophers: God hath this report that being in his first disposition that it cureth the Leprosy and many other vertues, this is not except by its compleat disgestion because the excellency of the fire acting in it consumeth all evil humours that are in sick bodies as well in hot as cold causes, But silver can not do this because it hath not so much superfluity of fire and is not so much disgested and decocted with natural

ma-

maturity, yet notwithstanding this it hath fierines occultly and vertually in it, but not so fully because the fire causeth not such Elemental quallities as in gold. And therefore silver being in his first disposition doth not cure the Leprosy so potently unless it be first digested by Art untill it have the cheif degrees of gold in all maturity. Wherefore other sick metallick bodies more weakly cure infirmities according as they differ more from them in perfection and maturity some differ more some less, which is by reason of the sulphur infected feid and burning of which they were made at the beginning in their generation and coagulation and therefore they cure not whereas the fire in them is burning and so infected with the Elementall feces with the mixture of other Elementall quallities.

Seeing therefore that gold is of such vigor amongst the vulgar and that being in his first disposition what wonder is it if it being brought into medicine ( as is experienced ) by Art and his vertue be subtiliated by digestion of decoction and purgation of the quallities but it may then cure more nay infinite or all diseases.

It makes an old man young and revive, it preserveth health strengtheneth nature and expelleth all sicknesses of the body it driveth poyson away from the heart it moysteneth the Arteries and breifly preserveth the whole body sound.

In the *Ludas purorum* it is thus written of the
ufe of this medicine the manner of ufeing it
according to all the Philofophers is thus, if you
will ufe to eat of this medicine then take the
weight of two florence Duccats of our Elixir
and one pound of any confection, and eat of that
confection the quantity of one dram in win-
ter. And if you do thus it driveth away all
bodily infirmities from what caufe foever they
proceed whether hot or cold, and conferveth
health and youth in a man, and maketh an
old man young, and maketh gray hairs to fall,
it alfo prefently cureth the *Leprofy,* and dif-
folveth Flegm mundifieth the bloud it fharpen-
eth the fight and all the fenfes after a moft
wonderful manner above all the medicines of
the Philofophers.

To which purpofe we thus find in the *Ro-
fary* of the Philofophers, In this (that is to fay
in the Elixir) is compleated the pretious gift
of God, which is the *Arcanum* of all the
Sciences in the world, and the incomperable
treafure of treafures (for as *Plato* faith) he that
hath this guift of God hath the dominion of
the world ( that is to fay of the Microcofme)
becaufe he attaineth to the end of Riches and
hath broke the bonds of nature, not onely, for
that he hath power to convert all imperfect
mettalls into pure gold and filver, but rather
becaufe he can convert and preferve both
man and every Animall in perfect health.

To this purpose speaketh *Geber, Hermes Arnoldus, Raymundus, Lullius, Ripley, Penotus, Augurellus, Aegidius, Valescus, Roger Bacon, Scotus, Laurentius, Ventura*; and diverse uncertain Authors.

Lastly, I now come to the generall consent of all the Philosophers and repeat what is found in their writings in the Book *de Aurora consurgeat*, and in *Clangor Buccina*, It is to be noted that the Antient Philosophers have found 4 principal effects or vertues in the glorious repository of this treasure.

1. First, it is said to cure mans body of all infirmities.

2. Secondly, to cure imperfect mettalls.

3. Thirdly, to transmute base stones into pretious gemmes.

4. Fourthly, to make Glass malleable.

Of the first. All Philosophers have consented that when the Elixir is perfectly rubified it doth not onely work miracles in solid bodies but also in mans body of which there is no doubt, for being taken inwardly it cureth all infirmities, it cureth outwardly by unction. The Philosophers also say, if it be given to any in water or wine first warmed it cureth them of the *Phrensy, Dropsie,* and *Leprosy,* and all kind of *Fevers* are cured by this Tincture and taketh away whatsoever is in a weak stomack it bindeth and consumeth the Flux of peccant humours being taken fasting it driveth away malencholly and sadness of the mind it cureth the infirmities of the eyes and dryeth up their

Moist-

moiftenefs and blearedneis, it helpeth the pur-
blind, red or blocdfhot eyes it mollifieth the
primy or web the Inflamation of the eyes and
all other incident difeafes are eafily cured by
this Philofophical medicine.

It comforteth the heart and fpiritual parts
by taking inwardly it mittigateth the pain of
the head by anointing the temples therewith
maketh the deaf to hear and fuccoreth all pains
of the ears it rectifieth the contracted Nerves
by unction, it reftoreth rotten teeth by wafh-
ing alfo all kind of impofthumes are cured with
it, by oyntments or emplaytors or injecting the
dry powder therein.

It cureth Ulcers wounds Cancers Fiftulas
*noli me tangere,* and fuch like difeafes and ge-
nerateth new flefh if it be mixed with corrupt and fower wine it reftores it, it expelleth
poyfon being taken inwardly it alfo killeth
wormes if it be given in powder it taketh a-
way wrinkles and fpots in the face by anointing therewith and maketh the face feem young,
it helpeth women in travail being taken inwardly and bringeth out the dead child by emplaifter,
it provketh Vrine, and helpeth generation
it preventeth drunkennefs, helpeth the memory,
and Augmenteth the radical moifture it ftreng-
theneth nature and alfo Adminiftreth many
other good things to mans body.

2. Of the fecond it is written that it tranfmu-
teth all imperfect mettals in colour fubftance laft-
ing weight ductibility melting hardnefs and foft-
nefs

2. Of

3. Of the third, that is to say of tranſmuting baſe and ignoble ſtones into pretious gems, I will not ſpeak of in this place, becauſe I have reſerved it for another place, that is to ſay the third Book.

Of the fourth it is writ that it maketh glaſſe malleable by mixture (that is to ſay of the powder of the white corporeal Elixir) when the glaſs is melted. Thus far *Aurora Conſurgens* and *Clangor Buccina.*

Now if you deſire to make pure and clear malleable glaſs learn this of me, and beware of what glaſs you make your mettal for you muſt not take glaſs of Flints, wherewith glaſs of windows are made but ſuch as your *Venice* glaſs is made of, and that is to be choſen out of the firſt mettal of the glaſs, which hath ſtud molten in the fire, in the glaſs makers furnace the ſpace of a night & then it will be without ſpots and pure therefore take as much of the ſaid glaſs out of the furnace with your Iron rod, as you have a deſire to convert, and when it is cold weigh it, and melt it by it ſelf in a pot, and when it is well molten project your white corporeal Elixir upon it and it will be converted into malleable mettal and fit and apt glaſs for all Gold Smiths operations. And thus is glaſs made malleable and prepared for any uſe but if this were done with the red Elixir it would be much more during, for there is nothing more pretious of which we will not now ſpeak.

Therefore Son or or Reader whoſoever thou art who readeſt my Books give credit to me and beleive me, becauſe all things that you ſhall find

writ

writ here are either the moſt approved writings
and collections of all writers or the Authors own experiments. For I have tryed many things and found many things true.  I beleive
no man liveth amongſt Mortals that knoweth
more ways of prepartions which are conccaled
by almoſt all the Philoſophers.

For that which perfecteth the great work that
they have all concealed which truely is the errour
of all Artiſts.  And this is all I would have you
to do. To calcine, diſſo've and ſeperate the Elements after join them together putrifie them or
reduce them into ſulphur ferment, project, Augment in vertue and quantity.  This is onely the
work of the Philoſophers of which the whole
Company of Philoſophers have writ in a conti-
nuate courſe,


*The  End  of  the*  Second Book.

*Hampaaneah Hammegulleh* :

OR,

The Rosie Crucian

# CROWN:

In which is set down the

Angels of the Seven Planets,
and their Occult Power upon the
Seven Metals , and miraculous
Vertues in the *Cœlum Terræ*, or
first matter of all things.

Whereunto is added,

A perfect full DISCOVERY

OF THE

*Pantarva*, and *Elixirs* of Metals.

By EUGENIUS THEODIDACTUS. Φιλότιμος.

*A Servant of God, and Secretary to Nature.*

*Ubi est scientia, ibi est invidia.*

LONDON:
Printed for the Author, and are to be sold at the
Rainbow in *Fleetstreet.* 1 6 6 4.

To the Worthy, Learned, Noble, and Valiant Colonel *Samuel Sandys*, late Governor of his Majesties Garrison in the Famous City of *Worcester*, and now one of the Right Honorable Members of Parliament, *&c.*

*Y*Our late respects to me have commanded my Soul to serve you : and knowing you are aswell a Philosopher and Learned, as a Souldier that can command Armies of Horse and Foot into good order for War; I therefore humbly present this little Piece of Philosophy to your pleasure : As the Book is Art and Nature united to serve you, so the Epistle may make you merry, by the great power of Natural things, for you know they not onely work upon all things that are neer them by their Vertue, but also besides this, they infuse into them a like Power, through which by the same Vertue they also work upon other things, as in the Loadstone, which stone doth not onely draw Iron Rings, but also infuseth a Vertue into the Rings themselves, whereby they can do the same : After this manner it is, that the common Harlots and Villains, grounded daily in boldness and impudence in Stage-Plays, infect all that are neer

them

*them by this property; whereby the spectors are made like them, therefore they say that if any one shall put on the inward Garments of a Stage-Player, or shall have about him that Looking-glass which they daily look into, he shall become bold, Confident, Ignorant, Impudent and Wanton; so a Cloth that was about a dead Corps, makes him that carries it sad and melancholy: And if you put a Green Lizard made blind, together with Iron or Gold Rings into a Glass Vessel, putting under them some earth, shutting then the Vessel; and when it appears that the Lizard hath received his sight, shall put them out of the Glass, that those Rings shall help sore eyes; the same may be done with Gold Rings: and a Weesel, whose eyes with any kind of prick are put out, it is certain are restored to sight again; upon the same account Rings are put for a certain time in the Nest of Sparrows or Swallows, which afterwards are used to procure Love and Favor: These observations and ten thousand more I made to serve you, and they shall testifie, you shall know you have power to command,*

Your most affectionate

humble servant

JOHN HEYDON.

# The third Book.

*Of Saturne or Lead the first Direction.*

## CHAP. I.

*Of the Elixar, Putrefaction into Sulphur, the
Oyl of the Sulphur, of the Conjunction of the
Salt and Oyl of the Spirit, or Salt of Saturne,
which containeth the Oyl or soul of the Menstruum of white Mercury and red water of Paradice, Resolution, Solution, distillation, Hyl,
Purgation, resolution of Sericon, of the Gum
of Sericon, of the solution of the Minium or
Adrop, of Calcination of Minium into Adrop
and red Lead, of Calcination of Lead with*
Aqua Fortis.

VEry many have writ of *Saturne* or Lead,
but none that I know of have writ fully thereof in any particular Treatise ;
therefore I do not here onely set down
what I have gathered from them most briefly and
truely, but also those things which I have found
and proved by my own experience, which I have
annexed to them, that the work may be absolute
and compleat.

Of

Of which, as they say, *Mary* the Prophetess, and the Sister of *Moses* in her Books of the work of *Saturne* is thus said to write, Make your water running like the water of the two Zaibeth, and fix it upon the heart of *Saturne* : And in another place, Marry the Gum with the true Matrimonial Gum, and you shall make it like running water. Of which process of Mary, *George Ripley* our Country man hath these verses.

*Maria mira sonat*
*Quæ nobis talia donat*
*Gummis cum binis*
*Fugitivum fugit inimis*
*Horis in trinis*
*Tria vinclat fortia finis*
*Fila Plutonis*
*Consortia jungit Amoris.*

   Or thus,

*Maria mira sonat, breviter qui talia donat*
*Gummi cum binis fugitivum fugit in imis*
*Horis in trinis tria vinclat fortia finis.*
*Maria lux roris ligam ligat in tribus horis*
*Filia Plutonis consortia jungit Amoris*
*Gaudet inassala sola per tria sociata.*

The heart of Saturne, saith *Ripley*, is his white and clear body, out of whose doctrine the work doth briefly thus proceed, that is to say, that a water he made out of the body of Saturne, like the water Zaibeth, and that water fixed upon the heart of Saturne; but because the practice of

draw-

drawing out this water of Zaibeth, doth not appear out of this, nor the way of making the heart of Saturne, therefore the foregoing direction in he *Holy Guide* will shew them both.

Therefore I have joyned two Tables, in one of which the shorter is the demonstration of the reduction of the body of Saturne into his heart or Salt, the other longer and greater, is the extraction of the water Zabieth; and the consummation of the work of Saturne.

Having thus described this work, I now come to the explanation, and say, that the Calcination of the Body is twofold; for the Calcination thereof in the shorter work, for extracting the heart of *Saturne*, is done on this wise by *Aqua Fortis.*

Take 8 or 10 Ounces of Lead in Filings, and dissolve it in *Aqua Fortis* in double proportion, and fortified with Salt Armoniack in an Earthen Vessel with a narrow neck, and set in ashes till it be totally dissolved; and there will remain a white matter in the bottom like Grains of white Salt, which is a figure of perfect solution; then pour your matter that is dissolved in the water into a body, and set thereon a Limbeck, and in Balneo draw away the corrosive water, till there remain a dry substance in the bottom; and so you have the body converted white by Calcination with corrosive water, out of which the heart of *Saturne* is to be drawn.

The way to wash away and purge the corrosive water from the body, pour warm water upon the substance in a Limbeck, and pour it often off till it have no sharpness at all upon the

tongue,

tongue, and then your body is prepared for drawing out the Salt.

When your matter is well dried, dissolve it a-it again in distilled Vinegar, and distill the Vinegar twice or thrice from it, and in the bottom you shall have a lucid clear and white shining Salt, which is then called the heart of *Saturne.*

Now I come to the practice of the other greater work, that the verity of the stone may be found, of which many have made mention in their Books, as *Raymundus*, who calleth it the Vegetable Mineral, and Animal Stone; *Geber* saith there groweth a Saturnian Herb on the top of a Hill or Mountain, whose blood if it be extracted, cureth all infirmities.

*Ripley* writ a whole Book, called his *Practical Compendium*, of the practice of the Vegetable Stone, teaching the manner and form of operation; but because he neither set down the solution plainly nor perfectly, he hath been the cause of much error, and hath not onely deceived me but all those that followed him, untill after a long time I found a way to dissolve *Saturne*, so that it could never after by distallation be turned into Lead again, which is the chiefest and greatest secret of the Vegetable Stone.

But let us hear the words of *Mary* the Prophetess, and *Ripley* taken from her: The Radix of our matter is a clear and white body which putrifieth not, but congealeth *Mercury* or Quicksilver, with its odor makes its water like the running water of the two *Zabieth* (*alis* Zubech) and fix it upon the fixed heart of *Saturne*: which
words

words do most aptly agree with the properties
of Lead ; for if any one be smit or wounded
with a Bullet, and the Bullet remain in the body,
it will never putrifie.

And also if Quick-silver be hanged in a Pot
over the fume of molten Lead, so as the fume of
the Lead touch the Quick-silver, it will congeal it.

Thus far of the preparation of Lead, we now
come to its denomination , They bid us fix the
water *Zaibeth* upon the fixed body of the heart
of *Saturne*; now for the expofition of the body,
for the name of *Saturne, Ripley* calleth it *Adrop,*
of which that is made which the Mafters call *Se-*
*ricon*; the water of *Sericon* they call their Menftruum, the two *Zabieths* joyned together in one
water, are the two *Mercuries*, that is to fay white
and red contained in one Menftruum , that is to
fay of the water and Oyle of the fixed body or
heart of *Saturne* : Follow what I have written
concerning the imbibition of the earth, our operation is no otherwife then in the Practical Compendium of *Ripley.*

*Ifaacus* alfo writ a Treatife of Lead, he worketh chiefly according to the doctrine of *Mary*
the Prophetefs , and laboreth much to fix the
earth of *Saturne,* and after to diffolve the body
in diftilled Vinegar ; that by the addition of cor-
roding and fharp things , his red Oyl may be diftilled, which he calleth the water of Paradice,
that he may imbibe his fixed earth therewith:
which way is much fhorter then *Ripleys,* but the
rubification and fixation of the earth is long and
uncertain ; wherefore I have both forfaken

*Ifaacus*

*Isaacus* and *Ripley* in making the earth , in stead
of which I have given the fixed heart of *Saturne,* as you may read in the *Holy Guide.*

But that the body may be prepared according
to this Table , and after my intention and the
desire of *Ripley* , we both will that the Oyl or
Water of Paradice be drawn out of the Gum of
*Sericon* ( whose father is *Adrop* ) *Sericon* is made
of Red-lead ; therefore it is first neceffary to
shew the way of making Minium of Lead, which
*Thomas Juc* an *Englishman* hath described, together with the Compofition of the Gum of *Sericon,* which Author I purpose to follow, as being
the best.

Take ten or twelve pound of Lead, and melt it
in a great Iron veffel, as Plumbers ufe to do, and
when it is molten, ftir it ftill with an Iron Spatula
till the Lead be turned to powder, which powder
will be of a green colour ; when you fee it thus,
take it from the fire and let it cool, and grind that
powder upon a Marble till it be impalpable,
moiftening the powder with a little common
Vinegar, till it be like thick honey, which put into a broad Earthen Veffel, and fet it on a Tre-
vet over a lent fire, to vapor away the Vinegar
and drie the powder , and it will be of a yellow
colour ; grind it again and do as before , till the
powder be fo Red as Red-lead, which is called
*Adrop* : And thus is *Saturne* calcined into Red-
lead or Minium.

Take a pound of this Read-lead and diffolve it
in a Gallon of Vinegar, and ftir it with a ftick
three or four times in a day, and fo let it ftand in
a cold place the fpace of three days : then take
your

your Earthen Veffel and fet it in Balneo twenty
four hours, then let it cool and filter the liquor
three times; and when it is clear, put it in a body with a Limbeck thereupon, and diftill the
Vinegar fo long as it will afcend, and in the bottom the Gum of the *Sericon* will remain like
thick honey, which fet apart, and diffolve more
new Lead as before for more Gum, till you have
ten or twelve pound thereof.

Now give careful attention, for we now come
to the point and period of *Ripleys* error, for if
you put four pound of this *Sericon* to diftill in a
Limbeck, and from thence would draw a Menftruum, as *Ripley* teacheth, perhaps you would
have fcarce one ounce of this Oyl, and fome
part of a black earth will remain in the bottom,
and moft part of the Gum melted again into
Lead, by which you may know that the *Sericon*
is not well diffolved, nor as yet fufficiently prepared, that a Chaos may be made thereof fit for
diftillation, becaufe it is not yet well diffolved;
therefore in *Ifaacus* there is found a way of re-
folving this Gum with diftilled Vinegar, acuated
with calcined Tartar and Salt-armoniack;Where-
fore, faith he, if thou be wife, refolve thy Gum;
but I like not this acuation of the Vinegar, as I
may call it, I rather choofe to refolve the Sericon in *Raymund's* calcinative water, which is a
compounded water of the Vegetable *Mercury* or
fire natural, with the fire againft nature, as *Ripley* teftifieth, and it is more verified by *Raymund*
in his Book of *Mercuriis,* where he teacheth how
to diffolve bodies with his calcinative water.

I will reveal unto you this water, which is al-
                                                    moft

most unknown : Note therefore , that the vegetable *Mercury* is the spirit of Wine (insted of which we may sometimes use distilled Vinegar ) and that the fire against Nature is a corrosive water made of Vitriol and Salt-Peter.

Therefore take which you will , either spirit of Wine rectified ( or *Aqua Vita* ) or distilled Vinegar four pound, and two pound of corrosive water, and mix them together.

In this water thus compounded, resolve half a pound of Gum of Sericon in a circulatory , and set it in Balneo four or five days , and the Gum will be totally dissolved into the form of water or Oyl of a duskish red colour.

Then distill away the water in Balneo , and there will remain an Oyl in the bottom, which is then the Chaos , out of which you may draw a Menstruum containing two elements ; and this is the true resolution of the Gum of Sericon, in this water you may resolve so much Gum as you please by reiteration.

Take two pound of this Chahodical substance, and prepare it for distillation in naked fire or sand, and lift up the clear red Oyl, wherein both the spirit and soul doth secretly lie hid , which *Isaacus* calleth the water of Paradise, which when you have you may rejoyce , for you have gone through all the gross work, and come to the Philosophical work.

Therefore now proceed to conjunction, and joyn the white heart of *Saturne* with the red Oyl, as it is found in the Rosary.

*Candida succincto jacet uxor nupta marito ,* That is to say, the red *Mercury* to the Salt, if you proceed to the red work.　　　　　There-

Therefore take four ounces of the Salt or heart of *Saturne*, and as much of the red Oyl or water of Paradice, and seal them up in a Philosophers Egg, and so soon as they shall feel the heat of the Balneum, the Salt will dissolve and be made all one with the Oyl, so as you shall not know which was the Salt, which was the Oyl.

Set your glass in Balneo, and there let it stand in an equal degree of fire, till all your matter be turned white and stick to the sides of the glass, and shine like fishes eyes, and then it is white Sulphure of Nature; but if you proceed to the red work, then divide your white Sulphure into equal parts, reserving one part for the white work, and go on with the other part, and in a new glass well sealed up, set it in Ashes till it be turned into a red colour.

When your Sulphure is thus converted, imbibe it again with equal weight of its soul, dissolving and congealing till it remain in an Oyl, and it will congeal no more, but remain fixed and flowing.

This then is to be fermented with the fourth part of the Oyl of Gold, as is often mentioned before.

We have set down already before of the augmentation in quantity and quality, therefore it is not necessary to repeat it here.

We will now return to the white Sulphure before reserved, that we may set down the manner of the white work.

When you have your red Oyl or Soul, if you desire to make the white Elixir, set part of the said Oyle in a glass in Balneo to digest, then take

it

it out and put it into a body, and in a lent fire distill away the spirit or white *Mercury*, which you must try, that you may know whether it arise pure without water or not, as you do when you try the spirit of Wine, for if it burn all up, it is well; if it do not, rectifie it so often, till it be without any waterinefs at all; then have you rectified your spirit, wherewith dissolve your white Sulphure, till it remain fixed, and flowing, as you did before in the red work, then ferment it and augment it with the fourth part of the Oyl of the white Luminary or Luna, as you did the red, and it will be the white Elixir, converting imperfect bodies into perfect Silver.

### *A Corollary.*

*Ripley* divided the scope of this work into four operations, whereof the first is the dissolution of the body, the second, the extraction of the Men-struum and the separation of the Elements; the third is not necessary in our work, because we cast away the earth after every distillation, in-stead of which we use our Salt or heart of *Sa-turne*; the fourth is, that there be a conjunction of our Salt as is before described.

### *Hereafter followeth the Accurtation of the work of Saturn.*

The way of extracting Quick-silver out of *Saturne* is found in *Isaacus*, of which I know how to make a special accurtation with his water of Paradice, which I gathered partly from the
fore

forefaid Author and others; *Ripley* made his accurtation with Quick-filver precipitated with
Gold, and the imbibition with Corrofive water,
which I like not, becaufe the Elixir fo made will
be the greateft poifon, as himfelf confeffeth,
that it were better for a man to eat the eyes of a
Bafilisk; then tafte that Elixir.

But becaufe I defire to fet down this accurtation of Lead alone and his Elements, that no
ftrange body may be added to our Elixir, and alfo that it may be made a Medicine for all ufes; I
have found out the way of making alone with
the *Mercury* of *Saturne* and his own proper
Tincture; for I make a body of one thing which
is a fpirit, and make that Medicine with its own
proper fpirit. Read all the Philofophers, and you
fhall never find a word of this procefs, nor none
of the Ancients will teach thee how to make the
*Mercury* of *Saturne,* which that it may be briefly
done, this following work will fhew at large in
our *Holy Guide.*

# CHAP. II.

*The Medicine, Elixir, Fermentation, Imbi-*
*bition Precipitation, Quick-Silver, Saturne,*
*Lead, The Toad.*

MY great Grandfather *Chriftopher Heydon,*
faith in a certain Manufcript of his, *Levi*
*enim Arte norunt Alchimiftæ Mercurium currentem*
*conficere ex plumbo,* that is to fay, the Alchimifts
knew

knew how by an easie Art to make current *Mercury* out of Lead ; but what Art that was, neither he nor any of the ancients have shewed unto us, *Quærite, quærite,* saith the first Alchimist (so *Paracelsus* was pleased to say in imitation of him) *& invenietis, pulsate & operietur vobis,* that is to say, Seek and you shall find, knock and it shall be opened unto you ; which may rather seem to be the words of an envious Master, then the precepts of a Teacher. But having learned this, I learned to seek, that is to say to read; I read, I knocked, that is, I tried many experiments, although they were repugnant to doctrine and Philosophy, therefore although I almost despaired of that Art, yet because nothing is difficult to the industrious, by often knocking, at last I found it apart, by what means I attained to the Art of such a facility, that is to say, of making Quick-silver of Lead ; and when the process is read to the operator, it will be rather rejected then believed: but to the end this Art may be revealed as a great secret, I thought it necessary to speak first of the Instruments necessary in this work, before I come to declare the doctrine, which are three in number, that is to say, a Furnace, a Crucible and a pair of Tongs, as appeareth in the *Holy Guide.*

CHAP.

# CHAP. III.

*The Crucible, the Furnace, the Hole in the Top*
*of the Furnace, the Tongues, the Coals.*

LEt the Furnace be *D*, the place filled with
Coles E, whereunto put fire and when the
Coals are well burnt, so that they give a clear
flame and fire, take your Crucible A, well anailed
that it break not with the suddain heat, and put
therein three ounces of filed Lead, having twelve
ounces of *Mercury* sublimate well ground, and
Salt Armoniack six ounces mixed together, which
put upon the filings of Lead into the Crucible
A; and when the fire is strong and glowing hot,
take your Tongs C, and presently take up your
Crucible, and put it in B, the hole in the top of
the Furnace till you hear a great noise and buz-
zing, then so soon as you can ( least the Quick-
silver flie away with the spirits ) take away the
Crucible with the matter therein, and set it in an
earthen dish filled with ashes to cool; and when
it is cold strike the lower part of the Crucible, so
that the matter of the Lead may fall into an
earthen dish, and you shall find your Lead converted into Quick-silver.

This Crucible and Furnace is at large characte-
red in the *Holy Guide.*

This work is to be reiterated with new spirits
till you have a sufficient quantity of Quick-silver, with which proceed as followeth to precipi-

B          tate

tate this Quick-filver, that from a fpirit it may
be converted into a fixed body by fixation.

Take of this Quick-filver fo much as you
pleafe, and put it to precipitate in a round glafs
well luted, and fet it in afhes to the top of the
glafs: yet let us ftay here a while, that your un-
ftanding may be the more enlightened.

Therefore underftand that the intention of
this work is to fix the fpirit, which may fooner be
done with the fpirit of a fixed body, which before was Homogeneal with the body, and which
of its own nature defireth to joyn again with its
body.

Therfore nature requireth that fhe may be hel-
ped by Art in this work, to which the Artift con-
fenting, he adminftreth thereto the pure and defired metal, which it delighteth to adhere unto;
which metal is Gold, which is thus prepared, that
it be fooner parted by the Quick-filver and ftick
thereunto.

Take as much pure Gold as you pleafe, and
diffolve it in *aqua regis* mixed with equal part of
*acetum acerrimum*, or *Lac virginis*; then fet it
to digeft the fpace of a day, then put your dif-
folution into an Alimbeck, and fet it Balneo, to
diftill away the water as dry as you can, and do
thus three times, and the third time diftill it in
afhes, that the Salt Armoniack may fublime. Then
put diftilled Vinegar upon the matter remaining,
and after it hath ftood three days in Balneo, diftill
the Vinegar away in afhes, that all the fubftance
of the Salt Armoniack may fublime: and do thus
three times, always putting in new Vinegar, un-
till the Oyl of the diffolved Gold remain in the
bot-

ottom; then take of your Quick-silver three
mes so much as your Gold, and pour it upon the
olution of the Gold, that they may mix together
nd be united: then put your quick-silver with
ie solution in a round Glass stopped onely with
peece of Cotton, and with a stick put it down
very day as it doth ascend, and keep your Glass
i ashes the space of a moneth, till your quick-
Iver be turned into a red precipitate, then again
issolve it in new distilled Vinegar, till the whole
abstance of the quick-silver be dissolved, and the
Vinegar be coloured in a golden colour, then di-
till away the Vinegar in ashes, and again pre-
ipitate the quick-silver, which is in the bottom
if a Gold colour, into a red and fixed body; and
o have you the *Mercury* precipitate of *Sa-*
*urne.*

It remaineth now that the body be imbibed
vith its soul, that this being from a spirit redu-
ed into a body, may again imbibe its soul, that it
aay be dissolved therewith; therefore put it into
Glass, and add thereto equal proportion of its
oul or water of Paradice, and shut your Glass
vell the space of five days, till the body be dis-
olved with the soul.

Then dry it in ashes till it penetrate and flow;
nd when it is dried, try it upon a hot Iron plate
it be fixed and melt, if not, imbibe it again with
alf the weight of its water, and do so till you
iake it fusible and piercing by imbibing and
rying it, and when it will melt in the fire, and
enetrate, it is then the stone, and fit for fermen-
tion.

We have said enough of the manner of fermentation in the second Book, and therefore it is not necessary to repeat it here: and so after fermentation it will be the Elixir.

Then it is to be augmented and projected, as is before declared; and thus the work of *Saturne* is accurtated, of which *George Ripley* saith,

*Adrop* is the father of the stone, Sericon his brother, *Lympha* his sister, the earth its mother.

But if you desire to know all the secret of *Saturne* or Lead, I will set you down one process out of *Paracelsus*: when you have well prepared the heart of *Saturne*, saith he, take two or three ounces of that heart and grind it small with double weight of Salt-peter, and put it in a subliming Glass, with a head well luted to sublime, encreasing the fire by little and little as long as any thing will ascend or sublime; thus far *Paracelsus*: now if you find this true, *Ripley* will tell you what you shall do with it, in these words.

When by the violence of the fire in the distillation of the Gum of the Sericon, a certain white matter shall ascend sticking to the head of the Limbeck, like Ice, keep this matter which hath the property of Sulphur not burning, and is a fit matter for receiving form, you shall give it form after this manner by rubifying it in ashes, and when it is red Sulphur, give it of its soul, until it pierce and flow, then ferment it.

Here I have delivered unto you all the ways and manners of *Saturne*, which are found in any of the Philosophers Books: to the end therefore that the work may be compleated with a demonstration

stration of this word *Plumbum Philosophorum*, as appears in the Practical Compendium of *Ripley*, we say that the Philosophers Lead is not taken for Antimony but for Adrop , being converted into the Gum of Sericon.

It remaineth now that we in order treat of the third termination of this Book : therefore after we have done with *Saturne* , it is necessary to speak of *Jupiter*, *viz*. Tin : but because there are many other ways of handling *Saturne* besides those we mentioned , therefore we refer the Reader thither, seeing he followeth his footsteps ; for he is the off-spring of *Saturne* and naturally born from him.

---

# CHAP. IV.

### *The third Table of the Elixir of Iron.*

IT is not necessary to prefix a peculiar Table to this metal alone, because it is set down before this book , nevertheless I will here reckon up its parts and operations as followeth.

1. *Calcination.*
2. *Solution.*
3. *Seperation.*
4. *Conjunction,*

5. *Putrefaction.*
6. *Sulphur.*
7. *Fermentation.*
8. *Elixir.*

Exaltation or augmentation and projection is spoken of sufficiently in the former Books.

*Mars* being most earthly of all the Planets or bodies, it is not to be doubted but that it may easily be reduced into a body with little labor ; and therefore most easily converted into Salt, which is done by Calcination : therefore we will first shew his conversion into Salt.

Understand therefore , that hence ariseth a twofold consideration , that is to say, that it be calcined one way into its body or Salt , the other way that the body be prepared for solution by calcination.

The practice differeth but a little, for whether you calcine Iron for its Salt or its Menstruum, one onely manner of preparation sufficeth.

That is to say, that you take filings of Iron or Steel, as much as you please , and mix therewith equal weight of Sulphur in an earthen body with a Limbeck will luted thereto, then set it in ashes to sublime till all the Sulphur be sublimed from it, then dissolve the filings which remain in the bottom in *Aqua Regia*, and it will be converted into Salt , which will be cleansed from the said water, if you put thereon distilled Vinegar and distill it away ; do thus three times with new Vinegar, and you shall have a yellowish red Salt in the bottom, which then is a body to be joyned to the soul, which keep in warm ashes till you use it.

Now for the practice of Iron for dissolution, take filings of Iron or Steel, so much as you please, and put it in an Iron dish filled with Vinegar, and set it in the flaming fire the space of three hours, then take it out and let it cool ; reiterate this work four or five times, then
calcine

calcine it with Sulphur as you did before.

When it is thus calcined, set it to dissolve in a corrosive water, by adding equal weight of our *acetum acerrimum;* and let it stand till it have dissolved so much as it can in the cold, then set it in hot ashes, and let it stand there the space of four or five days, pour off the water and dry which is not dissolved; and again calcine it and dissolve it, and when it is dissolved, so as the water be coloured red, pour it out into a body, and keep it till you have dissolved as much calcined Iron as you please.

Then take all your dissolutions, and with an Alimbeck distill away the water in Balneo, and put distilled Vinegar upon the matter remaining in the bottom, and let it stand upon it in Balneo the space of seven days; then take out your Glass and filter the dissolution, and then again in Balneo distill off the Vinegar, and in the bottom will remain a thick Oyl of the Iron or Steel; but if it be not dissolved to your mind, reiterate your solution in *Raymunds* calcinative water, but it would be better if it were edulcorated with *Aqua vitæ,* drawing it away again in Balneo, and so you have your Iron dissolved into a liquor.

Therefore proceed to distillation, that there may be a separation, and distill it in an earthen Vessel in a strong fire, encreasing the fire as much as you can, and receive the oyl, or soul, or red tincture of *Mars* separated from the remaining feces by the nose of the Limbeck, which oyl is the most permanent tincture for colouring Sulphures for the red work, or for exaltation of all

Elixirs

Elixirs in colour, for it makes it tinge and colour higher.

When you have thus prepared the tincture, then proceed to conjunction, and work with the Salt before reserved, taking three or four ounces of the Salt, and equal weight of the soul.

Then seal it up and set it to putrifie in Balneo, and keep it there till it pass through all colours and be white, and then it is Sulphur of Nature.

Then take out your Glass and set it in ashes in a greater degree of heat till it be red, then dissolve the red Sulphur with its own soul, and again dissolve and fix it; dissolving it in Balneo, and fixing it under the fire, and so it is prepared for fermentation.

The fermentation is, as hath often been spoken of before, with the resolved oyl of the Sulphur of Gold in a fourfold proportion to the Medicine, that by the addition of the ferment, it may be made Elixir transmuting all bodies.

And note that this Elixir of Iron excelleth all other Elixirs, for it rubifieth more, and tingeth higher, and is better for mans body, for it prevaileth against the spleen, constringeth the belly and cureth wounds, it knitteth broken bones together, and stoppeth the superfluous Flux of the Courses.

CHAP.

# CHAP. V.

*The fourth Table of the Physical and Alchymical Tincture out of the red Lyon and Glue of the Eagle, drawn out from the Authors experience.*

IT is chiefly to be remembred how we first taught you to diffolve Antimony with our *acetum acerrimum,* which may be alfo well done if you diffolve it in our calcinative water, and after that Antimony is calcined which we fpoke of in the end of the fecond book; it is alfo to be remembred that in the end of the book I fpoke of the Glue of the Eagle in the fixth Table of the firft book; thefe being remembred, it is to be underftood that we attribute no other beginning to this accurtation, except that where before we took the blood of the red Lyon and the Glue of the Eagle when they were both deftroyed; we now joyn them found and not hurt together, that they living may mortifie and diffolve themfelves, which I have fitly called Corporeal Matrimony, or the Union, for in this wedlock they dye together, that they may be vivified in the Celeftial Matrimony; therefore it is not to be wondred if this Table differ from the other, for this pertaineth to the handling of fpirits, the other way teacheth the manner of making the Elixir of bodies; therefore we now come to demonftrate the foregoing Table.

Therefore that I may plainly reveal all things
unto

unto you, take Antimony well ground, half a pound, and as much Mercury sublimate, likewise ground, and grind them both togeth upon a marble, till you cannot know them one from another; then set them in a cold place, that the matter dissolving may drop into a Glass set underneath, for when the matters are well mixed together, then say, that they will both shortly be dissolved when the water is perfectly dissolved, it will be of a greenish colour and lothsome smell.

Put this water with the thick part with it into a Glass, and let it stand the space of three days in a fixatory under the fire, and in short time you shall see your dissolvedness of a brownish black colour, and after, that is to say, in the foresaid time it will be red, something higher then red Lead.

Dissolve this calcined matter in *Raymunds* calcinative water, and when you have dissolved it all into a red liquor or deep yelow, then is your matter brought well into its Chaos.

Put this liquor into a fit body with an Alimbeck and receiver, and by distallation separate the red oyl or the red Mercury from the white body which remaineth in the earth; and if any matter ascend into the head of the Alimbeck, despise it not, but trie if it be fixed; and if it be not fixed enough, sublime it till it be fixed.

Whereunto joyn equal weight of its soul, for the Celestial Matrimony, and always leave out the earth in the bottom if you have any sublimate fixed, if not, take the white earth remaining in the bottom, with which proceed as before is said, and joyn the white body with the soul; when

they

they are thus joyned or married, set them to im-
pregnate and revivifie in Bulneo, till it pass
through all colours, and at last be converted into
red, which then is the stone.

The manner of Fermentation, Augmentation,
both in quantity and quality, and projection, is
spoken of before in other works.

And thus Sons, Brethren and Reader, I have
delivered and opened ( and also have amended
many things) all the secrets of the Ancient Philosophers, whose writings were rather published
to conceal the Art, then to make it manifest or
teach it ; although it pleased *Hermes Trismegi-
stus,* the first writer of this Art, both to say and
protest that he had never revealed, taught, nor
prophesied any thing of this Art to any, exept
fearing the day of Judgement or the damnation
of his Soul, for shuning the danger thereof, even
as he received the gift of Faith from the Author
of Faith, so he left it to the faithful ; yet when
you read his writings, either in his Smaragdine
Table, or in his Apocalips, or his twelve Golden
Gates, and shall find nothing plain or manifest,
what will you think of such an Author ? Believe
me all the Ancients have concealed the secret of
their preparations in the gross work, although
they writ most famously of the Philosophical o-
peration ; therefore I have used my endeavour to
trye, for out of their writings I found that the
Elixir might be made of the Planets or Mettals,
and also of mean Minerals, which came more
neer to a metallick nature, then reading more, I
found a certain method amongst them all, as it
were with one consent or voice on this wise.

First and principally, that bodies should be made incorporeal, that is to say, discorporated, or discompounded, which then is called the Hyle or Chaos.

Secondly, That out of this Chaodical substance, which is one thing, three Elements, should be separated and purified.

Thirdly, That the separated and purified elements should be joyned, the man and the woman, the body and the soul, heaven and earth, with infinite other names so called, that the ignorant might think they were diverse, which onely were nothing else but water and Salt, or the body and spirit or soul, that is to say, white *Mercury* and red, which they joyned together that a new and pure body might be created in putrefaction, that a Microcosmical infant might be created in imitation of the Creation, that is to say, Sulphur of Nature.

Fourthly, That it should be fed with Milk, that is to say, with its own proper Tincture, and after nourished by Fermentation, that it may grow to its perfect strength.

Having learned these, I begun to practice, and in the practice of every body and spirit, I found diverse errors; but reading more and trying more, at last I found the manner and true way of dissolving all bodies, separating and conjoyning them; finding the composition of their secret of secrets, that is to say, *Lac virginis*, or *Acetum acerrimum*, and *Raymunds* calcining water, wherewith I dissolved all bodies at pleasure, and perfected the gross work; wherefore I purposed, contrary to the custome of the Philosophers, and truely writ, that the Artift need to read no books but mine, for herein is almoft all things contained, which are found plainly writ by the Philofophers; and alfo thofe things which are found true by my own experience.

Now you have all things methodically in this Art without error, with which by the help of God, you may attain to the end.

Alchymy revealeth and openeth unto us four other fecrets.

The firft is, the compofition of Pearls, far greater and fairer then natural ones, which cannot be perfectly done without the help of the Elixir.

The fecond is the manner of making precious Stones of ignoble ones, by the fame Art which we taught before in malleable Glafs.

The third is the manner of making artificial Carbunckles in imitation of natural ones, which few or none have fpoken of.

The fourth is the manner of making Mineral Amber, of which *Paracelfus* hath onely writ in his book of vexations of Philofophers, and in the laft Edition of his works in the fix *of his Archidoxes* : but becaufe they cannot be made without the help of the Elixirs, therefore they deferve a place amongft the Elixirs; of the fourth, that is to fay; of the vertue or rather the vice of making Amber, I fhall handle it coldly : I have referved the explanation of this Ænigma, till the laft

place,

place, wherefore it is said, that the Elixir is perfected in the Decimal number.

---

# CHAP. VI.

*The fifth Table, of making of Pearls.*

THis Table of making Pearls, consisteth of
these parts, that is to say,

> *Lac Virginis.* Hydrochloric Acid
> *Dissolved Pearls,*
> *Quick-silver,* And
> *The White Elixir.*

Take *Lac Virginis*, or *Acetum Acerrimum*, so
much as you think sufficient for dissolving the
Pearls, as in double proportion to the Pearls;
as if there be three ounces of the Pearls, let
there be six ounces of *Lac Virginis*, wherein
dissolve the Pearls, and let the Glass in Balneo
to digest the space of a day, then pour out the
solution, and distill it in Balneo, and in the bottom of the Glass you shall find the thick Oyl of
the Pearls, whereunto add so much of your white
corporeal Elixir as sufficieth to make the matter
like paste, and put thereto equal weight of the
Pearls of Quick-silver; if the matter be too
thin, put more powder of the Elixir, if it be too
thick, add more *Lac Virginis* or Quick-silver, till
it be like Liver; grind this mass upon a stone till
it be brought to a fit thickness.

Then

Then make it up in what form you pleafe, therefore it is neceffary that you have a pair of Brafs or Iron Moulds in readinefs (but it would be better they were of Silver ) of what form you will, and fill them with this matter while it is foft; then peirce them through with a needle, or fuch like thing, and put as many of thefe in a Glafs as you will ( but firft hang them upon a thred ) and clofe well the Glafs, and bury it with the Pearls therein two foot under the earth, and let it ftand there the fpace of fix months till they be congealed with the cold into a fhining and clear fubftance like natural Margarites. Thefe Pearls made and compounded in this manner, are no lefs then natural ones, but much greater and more excellent by reafon of the white Elixir.

## CHAP. VII.

*The fixth Table of the Magiftery of Carbunckles.*

WE now come to fpeak of Carbunckles, which have their birth or original in the pits, and Golden Mines of the earth, of the fpirit of Gold and Mineral Salt indurated and corporeal, being decocted and difgefted into the hardnefs of ftone by the Archeus of Nature, as well by the heat of the Climate, as by the great heat of the Snn ; for they arife from the fpirit of the Minere of *Sol* or Gold under the earth, by whose influence they shine, as also from the hard Mineral Salt, by the mixture of which they are hardned into the nature of stone; whence the Philosopher intendeth and endeavoureth as near as he can to imitate nature by Art, and to make and compound artificial Carbunckles above the earth, with the same materials which Nature formeth them of under the earth; therefore he useth the same principles, operating with the spirit and soul of *Sol* undivided, and the most hard Salt of the earth, whereof *Venice* Glass is made, which two are the material Organs for Manuals: three things are required, that is to say, a Glass-maker, Furnace, a flaming fire, and a Crucible.

We now come to the materials, which are two, and are to be joyned together; the first giveth the form, the other receiveth it: that which giveth the form is the spirit and soul of *Sol* or Gold joyned together in the red Elixir, and is the agent, as it were the man; that which receiveth the form, is the hardest Salt of the earth contained in Glass, and is the patient, as it were the woman; the agent is the power of heaven impregnating the earth, the patient is the power of the earth, retaining the impression of the heaven.

Having thus demonstrated the Theory, we now lay the foundation of the practice, which are two, whereof the first is the preparation of the Elixir, the other of the Glass.

Therefore your red corporeal Elixir is to be dissolved with the oyl or tincture of *Mars* or Iron, because it hath the greatest vertue above

all

all other bodies, by whose Cœlestial power the
Earth, that is to say the glasse, is brought to the
hardnesse of stone, and converted into a stone :
And so the *Elixir* is prepared for projection upon glasse; but for the preparation of glasse there
is no more required but that it be made of the
same matter that *Venice*-glasse is made of ; the
composition of which if you know not, Take as
much *Venice*-glasse as you please, and weigh it
exactly, upon which project your *Elixir* : when
you have so done, put your glasse in the Crucible
to melt ; and when it is well molten, then take
your Corporeal red *Elixir* dissolved as before ( or
if you will, undissolved ) as much as sufficeth to
tinge the molten glasse, and put it tied up in a pa-
per into the Crucible upon the molten glasse ;
stirring it a little with a rod ; and there let it stand
the space of one hour : then take out the Crucible, and pour the matter into an ingot, and it will
be malleable, but as hard as glasse, and stonelike
to the sight : and you may either cut it like a
stone ; or work it with a hammer.    This Car-
bunckle-stone or metal hath the property of a
Carbunckle in shining and glistring above all natural Carbuncles ; and if it touch a Toad or Spi-
der, they presently die, because it taketh virtue
from the *Elixir* against all poyson : And if the
sick carrie this Carbunckle about him, so that
it doth touch the region of his heart, it takes a-
way the Cardiack passions, and diminisheth the
strength of the disease.

1 - Purple of Cassius

2 - Gold  C

3 - Powdered quartz

CHAP.

fire

# CHAP. VIII.

*The seventh Table denoting the composition of Minerall Electrum or Amber, as well naturall as Artificiall; and also speaketh of a Bell made of Amber used by* Tritemius.

HAving finished thefe two Secrets, we now come to the *Electrum :* but whether it is to be reckoned amongft ftones, or amongft bodies, it may be doubted; becaufe in the *Weft-Indies* it is found writ in the Spanifh Decads of the vertue thereof; it is affirmed to be the greateft Antidote againft all poyfon, and far more noble, then Gold : but if it be a metal, it muft neceffarily be the chief and fupreme of all metals; for other metals have their original from Sulphure and Mercury, but this metal confifteth of feven metals, and is the beft of all thofe which grow in the *Archæas* of the Earth. For where Gold is taken for the moft noble of all metals by reafon of its perfect digeftion and colour, this hath a greater degree of digeftion and colour, having a higher colour, that is to fay, clear red, approaching neerer to the true colour of the Sun. For as Gold is the Sun of other metals, fo this *Electrum* is to Gold as the Heaven to the Sun, wherein Nature as it were in Heaven hath created certain ftars fhining with clear beams of a Silverifh colour, fhewing plain to the eye that it confifteth of red and white metals mixt in the higheft degree of digeftion.

On

On the Contrary it may be objected,

*Ob.* 1.  That there are onely six metallick bodies , amongst which this is found to be none ; therefore it is rather <u>a Spirit</u> then a body.

Also thus.

*Ob.* 2.  The minere of every body or metal is converted into metal by fusion , but the minere of *Electrum* in melting always remaineth ; therefore it is no metal.

Otherwise thus :

*Ob.* 3.  There is nothing generated in the earth but stones, spirits, metals, or mean minerals : but *Electrum* is none of these ; therefore it seems to be no mineral.

1.  To the first objection it is thus answered. We say, that it is not apparent out of the books of any of the antient Philosophers ; that they ever dreamed of this natural and mineral *Electrum.* But more to the purpose :  <u>those are called Spirits, which flie from the fire</u> ;  but the *Electrum* flieth not from the fire : therefore it is no Spirit, is Quicksilver and the rest, and also mean minerals.

2.  We now come to the next.  We grant that the minere of every metal is converted into metal by the fire , which consists of Mercury and Sulphure.  This Axiome is evident in those metals which are imperfect , and flie from the fire either in their minere or in themselves, after they be reduced into metall ; and also the Gold minere , although before melting it flie from the fire , before the Gold be molten and converted

C 2                                    into

into metal ; yet becaufe Gold never flieth after it be molten , but is found fixed in all probation, therefore it is accounted the worthieft of all metals which confift of Sulphur and Mercury.

3. Now to the third, I fay, that I think it rather is of a ftony and metallick nature joyned together ; by which mixture it differs from a ftone, and alfo from metal : but becaufe it confifteth of Mercury, Earthly Salt and Sulphur mixed , therefore it gets unto it a mixt nature of them ; fo that it is half ftone, half metal.

Wherefore it is to be judged that it confifteth of three natures mixed together ; that is to fay, mineral, metallick, and ftony ; and is the beft of all thofe which grow in the Archeas of the Earth : for it exceeds mean minerals in fixation and conftancy , becaufe they paffe away in fume by long melting, and vanifh to nothing ; or elfe they melt eafily in moyfture,as falts,&c. But this *Electrum* or Amber remaineth fixed and conftant as well in the fire as water.

It exceeds metals in digeftion, colour and dignity.   In digeftion , becaufe it is endewed with the figne of greater and more perfect digeftion : for as Gold is more yellow by reafon of his greater heat and more perfect digeftion ; So this *Electrum*,becaufe it hath a higher colour then Gold hath, therefore it is more digefted in colour : for as Gold exceeds other metals in colour , fo *Electrum* exceeds Gold ; for Gold is yellow , but *Electrum* red,which is a higher colour then yellow. And as Silver is the *Luna* of white metals , fo Gold is the *Sol* of red metals : So *Electrum* is to Gold, as the heaven is to *Sol* in dignity or value :

for

for by how much Gold is more noble then Silver,
so much this *Electrum* is more noble then Gold.

Lastly, it excels stones in shining, and vertue.
In shining, because they shine by reason of
their hardnesse; so this *Electrum* sheweth many
sparkes, not by reason of its hardnes, but by reason of his compleatnesse. And as the heaven is a-
dorned with Stars, so this *Electrum* with spark-
ling, because it hath the clearness and brightnesse
of all metals. And as the Heaven containeth all
the Stars and Planets, so this *Electrum*, which is
the Heaven of metals, containeth the Sun and
Moon, and the rest of the Planets in it self; Gold
and Silver as it were the greater Luminaries, the
other bodies or metals as the rest of the Planets,
mean minerals as Stars in vertue. For although
many stones have singular properties and vertues;
so that some help the sight, others the Spleen,
some the Heart; some stop blood, some hinder
abortivenesse, some hasten childbirth, some resist
poyson: yet there is no one found which takes
away all infirmities, as *Electrum* doth, more then
all mean minerals, metals or stones, according to
his threefold conjunction, that is to say, Mineral,
Metallick, and Lapidifick.

Therefore whatsoever others please to think of
this Natural *Electrum*, this seemeth most probable
to me, that it is not simply a metal; but of a nature exceeding metal: for whereas stones, mean
minerals and metals are generated of Salt, Sulphur and Mercury, this *Electrum* takes his original from Stones, Minerals and Metals: from
Stones it takes *Salt*, from Minerals *Mercury*,
from Metals *Sulphur*. These three being brought

into

into one by the Archeas of nature, are its Elements, from a greater vertue and power of nature; which Elements have formed a higher degree of perfection then in any other ftone, mineral or metal, as it were by the Commandment of God Nature fhould afcribe a Crown of vertue and dignity above all minerals.

But however it be, it is taken two manner of ways amongft the later Magitians and Alchymifts, that is to fay, that which is made naturally, and artificially; naturally is that which groweth in the natural Archeas of the Earth; the Artificial is that which is made by Art above the Earth in imitation of Nature.

Whence *Paracelfus* a worthy Mafter in Magick feeing fully the nature of it, and the utility of Alchymy, commanding to make the *Elixir* thereof when as its natural body cannot be had, in his booke of *the Vexations of Philofophers,* and the fixth of his *Magical Archidoxes,* teacheth to compound an Artificial *Eleltrum,* that the Elixir muft be made thereof, as appears more at large in the faid Bookes; which I like not at all. He teacheth how to make the *Elixir* out of *Eleltrum*; I contrarily, the *Eleltrum* out of the *Elixir*: he would make the *Elixir* of the vertue of the *Eleltrum*; and I the *Eleltrum* of the vertue of the *Elixir*. I leave his way to his own followers, but I defire mine not to weary and vex themfelves in fuch a weak, but a more ftrong principle.

I make two kindes of *Eleltrum* one way; the firft whereof is Spiritual, the other Corporeal. Firft of the former; after you have made your red

Cor-

Corporeal *Elixir* by projection, in the same
Crucible melt one ounce of Lead, and likewise
another of Tyn; and when they are hot, take the
Crucible from the fire, and pour therein one
ounce of Silver melted in another Crucible; and
when these three white metals begin to be cold,
take two ounces of *Mercury* well purged, and put
those two ounces of Quickfilver upon the molten
metall by drops : then increafe the fire gently,
that too much of the *Mercury* do not fume away :
then in three other several Crucibles melt Iron,
Copper, and Gold; of each one ounce, which
you muft have in readinefs molten.   And firft,
put your molten Gold into the Crucible, where
your four white metals ftand molten, and pour it
upon them ; then your Copper, and laft of all
your Iron, ftirring the whole maffe with a ftick,
that it may mix together ;  and let it ftand in a
melting heat the fpace of an hour : then take all
out that is melted in the Crucible, and confider
well the weight of it ; and according to the good-
neffe of your *Elixir,* make projection for medicine.  And thus you have created and compounded fpiritual *Electrum* of the weight of feven
ounces, confifting of feven metals ; which metals fo converted into medicine, will be the E-
*lixir* of *Electrum*, and an Univerfal medicine,
for you need not after regard upon what body
(or metall) you project it. It is alfo the chiefeft
medicine for mans body : for although three or
four of all the Difeafes of the Microcofm were
united together, yet they may be cured with this
one medicine. If you diffolve part of this in Spirit of VVine, and diftill away the fame fpirit in

B *al-*

*Balm*, and the Oyl of the medicine or *Elixir* remain in the bottome, as is taught in the second book, you shall have the chiefest medicine of life, and most Noble *Aurum potabile.*

Note that if your Iron melt not well, then dissolve your *Electrum* in the Oyl or Tincture of *Mars*, dissolving and congeling until it have imbibed a sufficient quantity.

But if you desire to make corporeal *Electrum*, when your medicine beginneth to fail to convert metals any more into medicine, then in like manner project your medicine upon your melted metals or bodies; and they will be converted into corporeal *Electrum* metallick and malleable; of the vertue of which as I do endeavour to write nothing; so also of its vice, or rather of the viciousnesse of those that abuse it, I will touch a little sparingly.

*Paracelsus* writeth, that *Virgill Hispanus* and *Trithemius* made a Diabolical Bell of this Artificiall *Electrum*, upon which when they would invocate Spirits (which they called by a more decent name of *Intelligences*)they writ the Character of what Spirit they desired; and at the third ring of the bell the Spirits obeyed their desires so long as they desired to talk with them; and when they would talk no more, they hid the Character, and by the reverse ringing of the bell the Spirits departed. He that will forsake God, and require knowledge, aid and assistance from the Devil, let him share with *Arbucell*, and with him descend to the Infernal Lake. But we that are true Magicians, or rather Philosophers, confiding in God the Father, and the holy Trinity, approving

of

of Natural and lawful Magick or true Philosophy, but accounting the supernatural altogether infamous and unlawful. And we require the
doctrine and wisdome of divine goodnesse, and
the holy Spirit, to whom be honour and glory for
evermore. Amen.

## CHAP. IX.

*The eighth Table, which explaineth the meaning*
*of the Philosophers when they speak of the*
*tenth Number wherein the Elixir is finish-*
*ed: And also sheweth the wonderfull secret*
*of the Animal stone, out of George Riply,*
*with two other of his Workes.*

WE now come to the Last Chapter of this
Book, wherein is declared what the Philosophers mean when they bid us finish the worke
in the tenth number : it is to be understood that
as out of the *Hyle* or Chaos four are divided ; so
out of the *Hyle* or Chaos of metals. Because
metals or bodies when they are dissolved into liquor, then they are contained in the first or one
number, which is the solution of the body, of
which by distillation is made two, (That is to say,
Heaven and Earth, the *Menstruum* and *Salt*) that
which remaineth in the bottome is the Earth or
*Salt*, that which is distilled over is the *Menstru-*
*um* and Heaven. And so you have *One, two.*
When the *Menstruum* is separated, it is divided
into Three, that is to say, into Water, Air, and
Fire:

Fire : Yet it is to be noted , that the Air, which is the first part of the water containing an aery diſpoſition , although it be in the form of water, yet it is reputed aer , by reaſon of the conſimili-tude of the quality; and after its perfect rectification , it is a tinging *Mercury,* and the white Spirit of metals.　In like manner is to be conſidered of the Oyl , which although it is not in the form of fire , but a liquor; yet by reaſon of its Ardent heat, it is called fire, and the Soul or red tinging *Mercury.*　And ſo there is *One , Two, Three.*

When there is a Conjunction of theſe three, that is to ſay, the air and water with its Salt or Earth, in putrefaction, theſe three are united into one quinteſſence , and are made a new body ; in which three are united in one Sulphur, which Sulphur is the true Philoſophers *Mercury :* and in making this white Sulphur , you have once turned the Philoſophers wheel.

But that the work may be perfected in the tenth Number , if you adde the fire which is the fourth Element , to theſe three concluded in the foreſaid unity, and rubified ; then if theſe four in a new Conjunction be putrified in a lent fire of aſhes, then it is the ſtone : for in this work it changeth colours again , and is converted into a red ſtone : and by this means you have joyned four into one, that is to ſay, 1. 2. 3. 4. make ten : And ſo the ſtone is finiſhed in the tenth number, becauſe you have turned the Philoſophers wheel twice, as *Ripley* witneſſeth thus.

*But yet again two times turn about the wheel.*

The

The stone is to be diſſolved again with tne fire, or Soul ſes Tincture, and dried again until it pierce and flow; then it is to be fermented into *Elixir* with the Oyl of the Luminary; and ſo you have turned tne Philoſophers wheel again, which is then called the medicine of the third order. Of the ſolution of this, *Ripley* hath writ theſe verſes, teaching the reſolution of the white and red ſtone before it be tranſmuting Elixir, calling them his Baſes, ſaying,

> *Do as I bid thee, then diſſolve theſe foreſaid*
> *Baſes witty,*
> *And turn them into perfect Oyls with our true*
> *water Ardent:*
> *By Circulation that muſt be done, according to*
> *our Intent.*
> *Theſe Oyls will fix crude Mercury, and convert*
> *bodies all*
> *Into perfect* Sol *and* Luna *when thou ſhalt make*
> *projection:*
> *That Oylie Subſtance pure and fixt* Raymond
> Lully *did call*
> *His Baſilisk, of which he never made ſo plain*
> *deſection.*

By which verſes it plainly appeareth, his Baſes were onely two Sulphurs, or two ſtones, which in another place he called his *Mineres:* and theſe mineres ought to be diſſolved by his Ardent water, by circulation of the Oyl or ſoul upon the Sulphur, until it become a ſtone: for in this place he takes both the ſpirit and the ſoul for the Ardent water, willing that the ſpirit and ſoul be admini-

administred according to their tinging natures,
for the resolution of the proper Bafis. And thus
have you the words of this Ænigma explained of
the tenth number; which seeing it is the end of
the Art, I have reserved it till the end.

It now remaineth that we reveal one secret of
*Ripley,* which was never spoken of by any Philosopher; that is to say, the manner of making
the Sulphur of Nature out of the Minere of the
Microcosm, which is mans blood, of which he
writ the whole practice in his book of *the twelve
gates,* but most chiefly in his *Medulla,* where he
teacheth its preparation and work more plainly.
And because I have proved it to be true, therefore
I tell it more confidently, because I desire to
write nothing of my own fancy, but that which I
have first proved. Hearken almost the last verses
which he writ in his *Twelve gates*:

*1. I never saw true work truly but one,*
*Of which in this Treatise the truth I have told:*
*Study onely therefore how to make our stone,*
*For thereby mayst thou win both Silver and Gold.*
*Upon my writing therefore to ground thee be bold.*
*So shalt thou loose nought, if God be thy guide:*
*Trust to my doctrine, and thereby abide.*

*2. Remember that man is most noble Creature*
*Of Earthly composition that ever God wrought,*
*In whom is the four elements proportioned by nature,*
*A natural Mercuriality which costeth right nought,*
*Out of his minere by Art it is brought:*
*For our metalls be nought else but our mineres two,*
*Of Sun and Moon, wisely Raymund said so.*

The

*The clearness of the Moon and of the Sun so bright,*
*In these two mineres descendeth secretly ;*
*Howbeit the clearnesse is hid from thy sight,*
*By craft thou shalt make it appear openly.*
*This hid stone, this one thing therefore putrifie,*
*Wash him in his own broth till white he become,*
*Then ferment him wittily.   Lo here is all and sum.*

Out of these onely words there are two points observed, whereunto the Author steereth :  The first is , that mans blood be put to putrefaction, that Sulphur may be made thereof.   The second is, that it be fermented wittily ;  As if he should say , the Artist should prepare it , that it may be fit for fermentation.   Thus far of the Theory ; Now we come to declare the practice out of *Ripley's medulla.*

Take Mans blood drawn out of the Veine in March, and of a Martial man the Author meaneth (as I think) of a Cholerick complexion ; and when the blood is drawn out of the vein , let it cool, that the Green water may be drawn from it , which is saltish : for as long as that saltish water remaineth with the blood , it will not let it putrifie, because the water preserveth the blood from putrifaction while it is in a mans body.

When it is thus prepared , put it in an Egge-glasse well closed, and set it in *Balneo* to putrifie, in forty days or lesse it will be black ; and so go on till it be white.   When you have your white Sulphur , divide it into two parts, and keep one for the white stone , and rubifie the other for the red work.   And so you have two mineres , of which it is said,

For

*For our metals be nought else but our mineres two*
*Of Sun and Moon, wisely* Raymond *said so.*

And so to the end of the verses, as before.
Yet here it is to be understood, that the Philosophers Sulphur is not mineral or metallick Sulphur, from which metalls grow under the Earth :
but it is a purified Sulphur drawn out of metalls
made by Art above the Earth : out of which and
the Mercury of the body the stone ariseth. For
believe me, I had never writ any thing of this Art,
except I had seen the Sulphur of the Microcosm,
and the perfect solution of other bodies and Sulphurs.

Now have you prepared your Sulphur out of
the minere of the Microcosm : If you be a Philosopher, proceed to the end, and conclude your
work in the tenth number : If not, you are not
born to our Philosophy ; therefore give the Sulphur *Mercury,* that the work may be compleat.

I believe there lieth not any Secret in the
Chymicall Art, which thou hast not truly declared and playnly taught. But to the end that these
things which we have spoken may be more sure-
ly committed to memory, we will repeat the ge-
neral process of the parts as it is described in the
beginning of this third book. And because there
is not one, but diverse handling of the bodies,
therefore the Table is divided into three parts ;
the middle whereof discribeth the process of imperfect bodies to the stone ; the other two teach
the preparation of perfect metals for fermentation of the stone of imperfect bodies.

*The*

*The manner of preparing imperfect bodies.*

CAlcination of the body.
  Solution of the body into *Hyle.*
Separation by Distillation.
Conjunction of the separated.
Putrefaction of the conjoyned.
Sulphur by putrefaction to the Stone.
Fermentation of the Stone to the *Elixir.*
Augmentation of the *Elixir.*
Projection of the *Elixir.*

Some make twelve parts, as *Ripley* and others,
who call them twelve gates : but because three
other degrees are contained in these, it would be
ridiculous to repeat them : and because the way
of both ferments , whether white or red , is the
same.

*The Table of Fermentation.*

CAlcination.
  Solution.
Putrefaction.
Sulphur.
Solution of the Sulphur.
Red ferment. *Aurum Potabile.*
Quinteffence. *Elixir vitæ.*

So likewife it is faid of Silver when it is prepared.

White Ferment. *Argentum Potabile.*
Quinteffence. White *Elixir* of Life.

Now the Radiant Sun of the Philosophers ariseth, which will drive away the dark Chimera's, and disperse the black clouds. Here the Ænigma's are opened, thistles and thorns are cut up and burned. Now Reader mayest thou safely walke in the Philosophers gardens, and gather most wholesome fruit. Here grow most fragrant roses both white and red. Here grow Vines bearing full grapes, of which is made the wholesome Nectar. Here are found trees of health and wealth, Trees of the Sun and of the Moon. Here spring two cool fountaines of Sciences and Knowledge sliding artificially through the garden upon the most pretious gems, and Silver and Golden Sands. Thou hast one field of Paradice given thee from God, that during the Life of his elect they may be kept in health, free from all sicknefs. Here the corrupt Nature puts on an incorrupt Nature. Here impure things are turned into pure things. Here are all diseases lost, and health encreaseth. Here the perfect unity and harmony of body dwell, and here is also all the most excellent treasures. Therefore let us always praise God for his gifts: let us worship him, obey him, love him, and beseech him to establish his grace upon us, and conduct us to eternity through all his ways of goodnesse, knowledge and faith, to Life eternal. Amen.

## *FINIS.*

www.ingramcontent.com/pod-product-compliance
Lightning Source LLC
Chambersburg PA
CBHW030602270326
41927CB00007B/1019